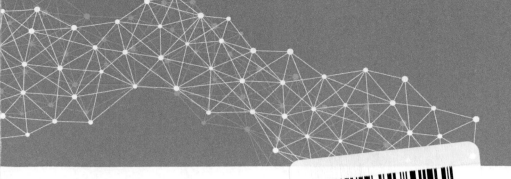

WIRED TO RESIST

The Brain Science of Why Change Fails and a New Model for Driving Success

Britt Andreatta, PhD

7th Mind
Publishing

 7th Mind
Publishing

This edition February 2017.
7th Mind Publishing
Santa Barbara, California

For speaking engagements please contact Jacqui Sneathen at Speaking@BrittAndreatta.com, or visit www.BrittAndreatta.com.

For order or bulk purchases of this book, please write Orders@7thMindPublishing.com.

Printing by Dog Ear Publishing
www.dogearpublishing.net

ISBN: 978-0-9973547-3-7 (paper)
ISBN: 978-0-9973547-2-0 (ebook)

This book is printed on acid-free paper.

Printed in the United States of America.

For my mom, Georgene Burton (1935–2016).
I am so grateful for everything you taught me.

TABLE OF CONTENTS

III. A New Model for Change + Transition: The Change Journey

IV. Thriving Through Change: Strategies for Success

V. The Path Ahead: Organizational Growth + Consciousness

Introduction—The Day Change Knocked Me on My Ass

I woke up to a text from my boss. "Don't go to LA. Cancel training. Come to HQ ASAP." There was no explanation and no details. My body had an immediate reaction. What had happened? Was something wrong? Or worse, had I done something wrong? I wracked my brain but could not think of anything. But that didn't quiet the knot in my stomach or the worry in my brain. So I got out the door as quickly as I could and began driving to the office. As usual, I turned on the radio, and to my surprise heard that the company I worked for at that time (Lynda.com) had been acquired by LinkedIn.

Wait, what?! I had absolutely no inkling that this was coming—and I even worked in HR, reporting to the chief people officer. I was clueless and confused.

But I was also excited. I had just seen LinkedIn CEO Jeff Weiner speak at the Wisdom 2.0 conference the previous month and had been very impressed with his values and leadership presence. After his talk, I turned to my friend and said, "I would love to work for that company someday." So as I drove to my office, my head was filled with positive thoughts like, *This is so great. What an awesome company to work for. I can't wait to be a part of it.*

I arrived at the office and went straight to my boss's office. She sat me down and told me about the acquisition. It was fast-tracked and would be complete in 30 days, one of the fastest transactions on record for a purchase of this size. I was getting a raise and a nice stock package and I would be part of the global Learning and Development team. At that moment, I was shocked but happy and excited too.

She then shared that while me and two other employees were receiving job offers from LinkedIn, the rest of our 50-person team would end employment the day the deal closed. While it's typical that core functions like human resources and finance have redundancy in an acquisition, I now felt sadness and frustration. I was losing so many friends and colleagues with whom I had worked closely for four years.

My boss wrapped up by telling me that the L&D team worked in Sunnyvale, five hundred miles away, and I would need to commute there, weekly to start, with the goal of working remotely as soon as things settled down. I would now report to a person I had never met. This added to my worry and sense of overwhelm.

This conversation took less than ten minutes, and yet it changed everything about my world. Literally, ev-er-y-thing. The projects I was working on stopped. The people I collaborated with shifted. The career plan I had crafted became obsolete. And the person who supervised me switched.

As the acquisition closed, I experienced more changes, from the email client and laptop I used to the benefits I received to the travel reimbursement policy. I had to learn all new systems to request tech support, track sick days, book conference rooms, and set quarterly goals. I had to learn the culture, navigate relationships, and support my new supervisor, all while trying to demonstrate my value.

My exploration into the neuroscience of change began three months later, as I watched myself and my colleagues experience things that were not accounted for by all the well-known models and theories about change—yes, the very models I had previously taught.

Now granted, I was going through one of the biggest change initiatives you can experience professionally—a sudden and uninvited change with no ability to plan for it. But I was still struck by how much the models couldn't account for what was happening. And I would be remiss if I don't point out that I was lucky because this change was one I was excited about and it left me employed and insured, unlike the thousands of employees every year who get laid off or fired.

But clearly, something was amiss in what we know about change, so I set off to learn more because my book on the neuroscience of learning had just come out and it was natural to carry over that research into the topic of change. I also knew there was value in dissecting change from inside my own experience because I would find lessons that would apply to other organizations.

What I discovered astounded me. Several structures in our brain are actually designed to protect us from the potentially harmful results of change. Humans are wired to resist change and we are working against our biology at every turn. It's well documented that every year 50 to 70 percent of all change initiatives fail. I believe that we can reduce that number significantly by working *with* human biology and harnessing the power of our brains to thrive through change.

This book contains the results of my research into the latest findings from a variety of academic and corporate studies as well as interviews with leaders from all kinds of organizations. I synthesize them into practical takeaways for you to use in your life. The truth is that change affects us every day, both at work and at home. Knowing how we are wired to resist change and, more importantly, how to overcome that resistance will serve you throughout your life.

This book is written for working adults everywhere. Whether you are on the leading or receiving end of change, you'll find useful tips and strategies you can implement today. In addition, I used this research to build new training programs for leaders, managers, and employees and they are proving to be exceptionally effective in all kinds of organizations and industries around the world. If you want to learn more, visit BrittAndreatta.com.

This book is organized into five sections:

I.   We'll begin by understanding what change looks like in today's organizations.

II.   Next, we'll dive in to the brain science of change and why it drives fear, fatigue, and failure.

III.   Then I will introduce you to my new change model that synthesizes all of the findings into an effective tool.

IV.   I will also share tips and strategies for employees and every level of leader responsible for designing or implementing change.

V.   We'll end with a look ahead to the factors that will drive change in your organization for years to come.

Take a Learning Journey

Before I wrote this book, I taught this content through workshops, keynote presentations at conferences and corporations, and through training courses I designed for leaders and employees. In a live presentation, I model best practices in learning design, based on the research of my previous book, *Wired to Grow: Harness the Power of Brain Science to Master Any Skill*.

Engaging with concepts in a personal way will help you understand and remember the material, and help you shift behaviors, so you do things in a new way. To replicate that for you here, at the end of each section you will find this light bulb icon marking a section called "Your Learning Journey." Each includes instructions for applying the content to your current or anticipated change experiences.

I recommend that you use these sections to build your confidence and competence around change. By the end, you will have a plan for implementing successful change and thriving through the chaotic effects of relentless change.

To make this easier, I have created a free downloadable PDF for you to fill out as you explore each concept (www.BrittAndreatta.com/Wired-to-Resist).

Tip: To maximize your experience, find a partner you can share this material with. Social learning actually boosts long-term retention, and when you work in partnership you both gain the insights of each other's experiences. So ask a friend or colleague who is also moving through change (hint: that would be anyone with a heartbeat) and explore together.

A note about the cover. In science, the symbol for change is Δ, or delta. When I was in college, we used Δ in our lab reports but it's also used in shorthand for note-taking to represent the concept of change or difference. In addition, the triangle is the shape of road signs that convey some sort of warning and it also represents a mountain that can be climbed. It seemed appropriate to riff on these concepts to convey the neuroscience of change, our biological resistance to it, and our ability to successfully move through a change journey.

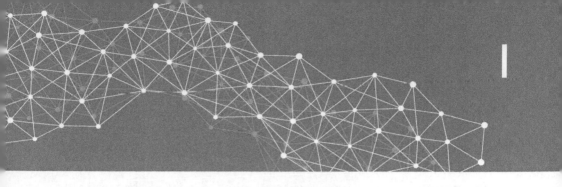

I

UNDERSTANDING CHANGE

1. The Costs of Change Gone Wrong

Failed change is costing trillions of dollars per year. Some of these failures are so spectacular or widespread that we all know about them. Consider the HealthCare.gov website or Samsung's Galaxy Note 7 smartphone, costing over $840 billion and $5 million respectively. Or consider JC Penney's epic rebranding misses or the demise of Borders bookstores after several strategic missteps. These failed changes made headline news for weeks.

Other equally expensive changes die a quiet death in organizations all around the world, known only by the people who work there. For example, one global pharmaceutical company invested millions of dollars to implement a new enterprise resource planning (ERP) system and still had not achieved success after three attempts. And a global high-tech company had to scrap an expensive overhaul of its performance review process after a last-minute change in executive support.

Failed changed initiatives affect every industry and every level of organization. They can occur in every function from marketing to human resources, from production to legal. It's estimated that 50 percent to 75 percent of change initiatives fail. Think about how astounding that is. Change initiatives are not just spontaneous whims thrown together by idiots. They are carefully designed, and expertly crafted by leaders and subject matter experts. Reports are written, data is analyzed, and rollout plans are built.

Even so, half to three-quarters will fail . . . expensively and sometimes spectacularly. Change can fail for a wide variety of reasons. According to McKinsey & Company, a global consulting company, there are three forms of failure:

- **Failure to launch**, which indicates that there was too much resistance to get the planned change off the ground

- **Failure to sustain**, which happens when a good idea gets launched but never gets sufficient adoption to become part of the day-to-day work or culture of the organization

- **Failure to scale**, which occurs when the change cannot transition successfully as the organization grows

Unintended Consequences

The cost of the failed change is not the only consequence. Failed change initiatives can generate a ripple effect that harms customer satisfaction as well as employee loyalty. In fact, mismanaged change, if it's systemic, can cause employees to lose faith in their leaders and the future of the organization. As a result, employees disengage and ultimately leave.

This is certainly an issue in the United States where the US Bureau of Labor Statistics is showing that there are now more job openings than hires, allowing employees more power to find a better place to work. But it's happening around the world too. According to a 2015 global study by Globoforce, a talent development company, HR leaders in all kinds of industries are identifying employee turnover and engagement as their top concerns.

Researchers have been studying the cost of employee disengagement and Gallup estimates that a disengaged employee costs $3,400 for every $10,000 in salary, or 34 percent. Gallup is known for its groundbreaking and global research on employee engagement. As described in their *State of the American Workplace* report, they have identified three types of employees:

- **Engaged:** "Engaged employees work with passion and feel a profound connection to their company. They drive innovation and move the organization forward." In the US, Gallup's study shows that 30 percent of employees fall in this category.

- **Not engaged:** They find 52 percent of employees are not engaged. They are defined as employees who "are essentially 'checked out.' They're sleepwalking through their workday, putting time—but not energy or passion—into their work."

- **Disengaged:** In the US, approximately 18 percent of employees are actively disengaged and are "acting out their unhappiness, undermining what their engaged coworkers accomplish." The financial cost shows up in tardiness, missed work days, decreased productivity, and shrinkage, which is a fancy word for stealing the office supplies and other resources.

	Company A US Offices	Company B Denver Office
Headcount	3,725	120
% disengaged (nat'l avg 18%)	671	22
Median salary	$150,000/year	$50,000/year
% cost of disengagement	34%	34%
Cost per disengaged employee	$51,000/year	$13,600/year
Total cost of disengagement	$34,221,000/year	$299,200/year

An example of calculating the costs of disengagement

When I consult with executives, I like to help them understand the real cost of disengagement. I build a slide that shows what Gallup's analysis means for their organization. All I need is their headcount and median salary in their organization and I can show them this compelling data (see two examples above). Using Gallup's data, I can also show the impact of disengagement in certain industries, like ad agencies, or in a sector like state or federal government.

It's estimated that disengaged employees cost organizations over $550 billion per year in the United States alone. But what about the rest of the world? Gallup's *State of the Global Workplace* report shows that 30

	Company C India	Company D South Africa
Headcount	500	500
% disengaged (nat'l avg)	160 (32%)	225 (45%)
Median salary	$15,000/year	$15,000/year
% cost of disengagement	34%	34%
Cost per disengaged employee	$5,100/year	$5,100/year
Total cost of disengagement	$816,000/year	$1,147,500/year

Costs of disengagement by region

percent of global employees are actively disengaged and the report has country- and region-specific data. In India, for example, 32 percent of employees are disengaged, and that number climbs to 45 percent in South Africa and dips to 14 percent in United Arab Emirates.

When leaders see the overall and real costs of disengaged employees, they get very focused on creating an engaging work environment.

What does change have to do with engagement? Quite a bit, actually. As you'll discover in future chapters, we are biologically wired for constancy and can find chaotic or rapidly changing environments to be quite stressful. While we might first respond by focusing and working harder, ultimately our brain will push us to check out emotionally, and even physically, becoming the sleepwalking and unhappy employees that Gallup describes.

We'll also learn that when employees can't find their way through change, they are more likely to quit. While losing a disengaged employee might be a blessing, the truth is that you're more likely to lose your best people. And replacing good people is much more expensive than leaders often realize.

Research by the Society for Human Resource Management finds that the cost of replacing an employee is 50 percent to 250 percent of their annual salary plus benefits. This takes into account the cost of recruiting and hiring a new person, the lost productivity of the role until it's filled, and the time it takes for the new person to get up to speed and fully productive.

The range of percentage is based on the employee's skill level. Entry-level positions will cost 50 percent of their salary plus benefits to replace while a position of leadership or high level of skill (for example, IT or engineering) will be closer to 250 percent. Again, this can seem very abstract so I find it helpful to calculate the true costs so leaders can see the real impact. Use data from HR and industry sources to create a sense of the real hit to your bottom line. The website Bonus. com has an online "cost of employee turnover" calculator that allows you to enter your data and see more details. Again, leaders are often surprised to see how much attrition is actually costing them.

It's not like people aren't trying to fix this problem. Hundreds of books have been written on managing change, and thousands of consulting firms offer their services. You can find whitepapers, articles, and blog posts galore, all attempting to crack this tough nut.

For example, consider these findings from consulting firm Willis Towers Watson's global survey on the ROI (return on investment) of change and communication involving companies from North America, Asia, and Europe:

- 29 percent of change initiatives launch without any kind of formal structure to support them
- 87 percent of respondents stated that they provide change management training to their managers but only 22 percent of organizations say their change training is effective
- While 68 percent of senior leaders say they are "getting the message" about the change, this drops to 53 percent for middle managers and 40 percent for front-line supervisors

Clearly, there is a lot of opportunity to improve our understanding of today's change. To date, few people are exploring the neuroscience of change and even fewer know how to translate that knowledge into actionable takeaways and leadership training. That is what I plan to accomplish with this book.

2. Change in the Modern World

There is no getting around change. It happens every day in every type of organization. But the nature of workplace change has definitely shifted over the last 30 years, driven by a few key factors.

First, the pace of technological innovation has increased. When you map our generation's advancements in technology on a timeline, the space between them gets smaller and smaller. And the time until 25 percent of the US population is using it gets shorter and shorter. Each innovation has the power to radically shift society, including how business is done.

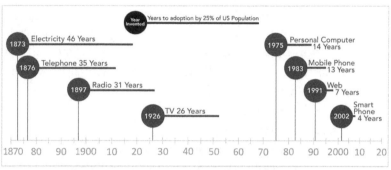

Adoption of new technology over time (source: Singularity.com)

Just think about how much your day-to-day work has changed with the immediate communication demands of email and websites. And how the widespread use of smartphones is pushing more demand for mobile access, so that you have everything you need in your pocket, 24 hours per day.

In addition, technology is big business, and innovation by the makers of computers, smartphones, and software creates a fast-paced, competitive market that drives unending upgrades and versions. If your organization has no change initiatives beyond keeping up with technology, you are still likely plenty busy with those.

Second, technology has enabled global communication and global business in a way that means that work is often 24/7, 365 days per year because, somewhere, you have an employee working or are trying to reach a potential client or supplier. Even if you are a small mom-and-pop business working traditional hours on Main Street, you cannot buffer yourself from all this change because it impacts your employees and customers.

Third, and finally, capitalism drives a relentless surge of growth and improvement. The market is filled with potential disruptors, especially because technology has made it so easy to create new businesses in this digital economy. For companies to survive, they must be striving for the newer/faster/better thing that distinguishes them from their competitors.

Change is constant, it is fast-paced, and it is relentless, much like ocean waves that pound on the shore. You might duck under one but when you look out, you just see sets of waves building and heading your way. Some might be small and others might be whoppers that can kick your butt if you aren't ready or don't have the right skills.

How does all this change show up in the average employee's life? It takes many forms in today's modern organizations. It can be a relatively small, like a new phone system, or sweeping, like a total redesign of the organization or its products. Employees experience a range of changes, such as these common change initiatives. Consider which ones have affected you over the past 12 months:

- A new job or role
- A new manager
- A switch to a different work station or work place
- A new leader of your function or organization
- A change on your team (the loss or gain of coworkers)
- A change in another department or team that affects yours
- A shift in a process, policy, or procedure
- An implementation of new or different technology
- A drive to capture a new client or market
- A move into a new regional or global territory with different cultures, laws, customs, and perhaps languages
- A merger or acquisition
- A geopolitical shift that affects the common market

These work changes may drive big personal changes as well: moving into a new home, settling in to a new neighborhood or community, and perhaps moving your kids to a new school.

You can see that change is happening in many ways and that we are actually moving through multiple change initiatives simultaneously.

Five Types of Change

While they can differ in size and impact, there are essentially five types of change. See if you can identify which types are at play right now in your organization:

1. **Strategic (how the organization will fulfill its mission):** This includes redesigning products or services and targeting new markets. For example, when LinkedIn added learning to its suite of services by acquiring Lynda.com. While the company had previously focused on helping professionals find opportunities and build their network, adding learning allowed them to help people close skill gaps to be more qualified for certain roles.

2. **Structural (the organization's internal set up):** This includes its divisions or functions, its org chart of authority, and administrative procedures. Changes might include reorganization of teams or departments, hiring growth that adds layers of hierarchy, or expanding locations. Every time furniture giant IKEA opens a new store within an existing territory or expands into a new country, they are making a structural change.

3. **Process (how the organization maximizes productivity and workflow):** This includes optimizing manufacturing processes, implementing new software to support sales, or shifting technology such as implementing a new email

The five types of change at work

system or mobile access. For example, when Coca-Cola, Stanley Black & Decker, and American Red Cross implemented Salesforce, they engaged in a process-oriented change.

4. **Talent (maximizing employee skill and performance):** This involves initiatives affiliated with every aspect of the employee lifecycle including hiring, supervising, coaching, and training. Many organizations are shifting how they do performance reviews. Adobe was one of the first to do away with the traditional annual rating process and many companies have followed suit including GE, Gap, Accenture, and Deloitte to name a few.

5. **Cultural (shifting the attitudes, values, and behaviors of people such as employees and customers):** This might include revising core values, branding, and marketing, and even how people engage with a product or service. For example, when Satya Nadella took over as Microsoft's new CEO in 2014, he launched an intentional cultural shift toward continuous learning and improvement, the principles espoused by Dr. Carol Dweck's work on the growth mindset.

But not all change is created equal. Large changes often include more than one of these types, creating a domino effect across the organization, and all can potentially impact others outside the organization—such as suppliers, customers, and shareholders— creating an intricate web of potential effects and consequences. Other changes may be small, and barely register as a blip in the organization. This got me thinking about what distinguishes one change experience from another and whether these differences might help us analyze change readiness or predict potential problems.

3. Change vs. Transition

My Identity

"Understanding your identity in Christ is absolutely essential for your success at living a victorious Christian life!"

Dr. Neil T. Anderson, *Who I Am in Christ*
(Gospel Light, 1993)

Satan's Lie	God's Truth
You are a sinner because you sin.	You are a saint (one declared righteous by God) who sins.
Your identity comes from what you have done.	Your identity comes from what God has done for you.
Your identity comes from what people say about you.	Your identity comes from what God says about you.
Your behavior tells you what to believe about yourself.	Your belief about yourself determines your behavior.

Dr. Timothy Warner, *Resolving Spiritual Conflicts and Cross-Cultural Ministry*
(Freedom in Christ Ministries, 1993)

Bookmark Front:
Dr. Neil T. Anderson, *Victory Over the Darkness*
(Gospel Light, 1990)

All references used by permission.
Please do not reproduce. Not for individual sale.

FREEDOM IN CHRIST
MINISTRIES

9051 Executive Park Drive • Suite 503
Knoxville, TN 37923
865.342.4000 | info@ficm.org

www.ficm.org
www.freedominchrist.com

...scs two large and very different ...e difference. On the one hand, ...structural; a thing you execute. It ...ge plan written with measurable ...then there is *transition*, the human ...hich includes humans' emotional ...ge and how motivated they are to ...ess, largely driven by our biology, ...ment rather than execution.

The Transition
Emotional
Reactive
Process
Adjustment

...rsus transition

...of *Managing Transitions*, argues that, ...hs make the big mistake of focusing ...a change plan without preparing for ...ansition.

...ransition is the reason so many change ...ire people to get on board and par- ...plans in the world cannot overcome ...nt, or downright oppositional.

...doesn't have to be this way. With the ..., leaders can be ready to successfully ...ore importantly, help their people do

Mapping Change Difficulty: Disruption and Acclimation

From all the various change initiatives I have witnessed in my years of consulting, I have consistently seen four factors influence outcomes. The first two:

- **Disruption:** How much disruption does the change create for employees? Some completely disrupt the day-to-day workflow while others have a negligible impact. So there is a continuum of disruption from very low to very high.

- **Acclimation:** The time is takes to acclimate or get used to the change is another factor. Some changes can be acclimated to very quickly (hours or days) and others can drag on for months or even years. This would be another continuum from very little time to a lot of time.

These two factors allow us to plot the impact of different types of changes into quadrants. Changes that are low disruption and require a low amount acclimation time fall into the bottom-left, or green zone: changes that are easy to adjust to quickly. For example, if you upgrade to eco-friendly lighting or if you switch to a different vendor or provider, employees might not even notice the difference.

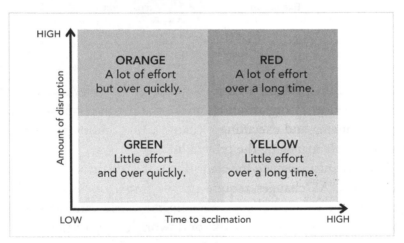

Matrix of disruption and acclimation

If a change falls into the bottom-right zone (yellow), it doesn't cause much disruption but will require stamina, since the adjustment period will take longer. For example, the slow preparation to meet a new regulation that goes into effect in two years.

The upper-left zone (orange) represents changes that are quite disruptive but are acclimated to quickly, such as converting to a new email and calendar system like Microsoft Outlook or the Google suite. Almost inevitably, changes that impact how people communicate, schedule meetings, and manage their time will be disruptive for a bit. Usually conversions like this are implemented over a weekend, although months of work were going on in the background up until the date of conversion.

Finally, the upper-right zone (red) represents changes that are high in disruption and time to acclimation. Examples include a complete revision of an organization's products and services, or a merger or acquisition with a company with very different values, leadership structure, etc.

This matrix provides a quick way to assess changes. For example, Facilities might decide that they need to switch the faucets in the bathrooms or resurface the parking lot. Depending on the situation, those things might fall into the green zone—unless the organization has limited bathrooms and parking spaces, in which case this change may require people to completely alter their routines (disruption) for many days (acclimation), putting these changes into the orange zone.

When working with leaders on change initiatives, I have them use this matrix to consider the impact proposed changes will have on employees. It's a good predictor of how much resistance and upset a change is likely to cause.

However, the change-difficulty matrix does not yet tell the whole story because two more factors play a significant role in how employees respond to change:

- **Individual choice:** Do the employees choose the change or will it be put upon them?
- **Desire:** How much do the employees want the change, or again, is it being put upon them?

These two factors are the most significant because they shape key psychological aspects of how humans are wired.

Mapping Employee Motivation

Choice and desire impact our emotions, attitudes, and motivations, as I am sure you have seen in your own experiences. It's easier to get on board with changes that you choose or want, even when they represent more disruption or longer acclimation time. Again, these two factors can be mapped against each other as a grid against "yes" or "no" for both choice and desire.

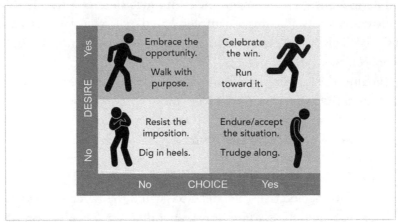

Mapping choice and desire

When you both desire and choose a change (yes and yes), you are likely to be happy about it and experience it with enthusiasm and energy. For example, you really want a job and you accept the offer. Your motivation would probably look like you running toward it and celebrating the win. Even though this awesome new job may represent quite a bit of disruption in your life and acclimating to it may take time, your motivation will be very positive, which is why we need both matrices to really understand change.

If you really want a change that you did not choose, you are likely to see it an unexpected but good opportunity. This is how I felt about the acquisition of my company—while I didn't choose it, I was super-excited because I was a big fan of the buying company and I really admired their CEO. My motivation looked like me walking toward it, feeling good about embracing the unexpected opportunity.

The next quadrant—a change that you did not desire but did choose—is tricky, and probably represents some kind of "should" or intentional sacrifice, like accepting a lower position rather than being laid off or relocating because it might lead to more opportunities down the road. These are a bit harder to get excited about, so motivation is lower because you are enduring or accepting the conditions. It might feel like you are trudging along and could include feelings of resentment or disappointment, even if you are trying to make the best of it.

Finally, in the fourth quadrant are changes that you did not choose nor did you want (no and no—or sometimes "Hell no!"). Obviously, without natural motivation you are likely to feel a lot of resistance toward this imposition, perhaps needing others to push or drag you along. Depending on how badly you feel about it, you might even actively fight the change, digging in your heels.

When you begin mapping change initiatives against these four factors—disruption, acclimation, choice, and desire—you'll find you have a much better way of predicting when people (employees, customers, constituents, etc.) are likely to resist. You will also have a better understanding of how much skill leaders and managers need to help people through the related challenges. An inexperienced or ineffective manager can probably do just fine leading an eager group through a green or yellow change. But it's going to require many more nuanced leadership skills if you have trudgers or resisters and are taking them through a highly disruptive change.

This assessment helped a chief technology executive completely revise his approach to change at one of the world's top research universities. He had been hired to accomplish a major shift in how technology services were provided across the whole campus, serving students, staff and faculty. In addition, he had inherited a team of experienced professional staff who had been in their roles for years.

He needed to roll out several major change iniatives over a three-year period, most of which would be disruptive, first to his team and then the various constituents they served. By mapping these four factors, he gained valuable insight that helped him shape the timing, messaging, and method for each of the initiatives. He also was able to define who needed what kind of training to best prepare them for success.

4. The Change Curve

The change curve is a classic model that has stood the test of time. I have found it a useful tool to help leaders understand the transition, the emotional aspect of change.

The change curve is built off research by Dr. Elisabeth Kubler-Ross, who studied death and dying. She found that people went through predictable stages of grief and acceptance when faced with a serious health crisis. Several researchers from different fields noticed that the model seemed to apply to all kinds of personal change situations. But the application to business occurred in 1990 when Dottie Perlman and George Takacs were studying change in a healthcare organization and realized that employees were exhibiting the same reactions Kubler-Ross identified. Finally, in 1998, David Schneider and Charles Goldwasser published a formal model for business applications in *Management Review*.

The change curve shows that change can be represented as a graph that maps time along the horizontal axis, and productivity and morale on the vertical axis. Before you initiate a change, the group or team is running along at their "normal" level of productivity and morale. This level could be higher or lower than other groups but it's their everyday state. Then the group moves through four stages.

Research on the change curve has shown that when introduced to change humans go through a predictable pattern of emotions. And a big part of leading change is being prepared for the emotions of the

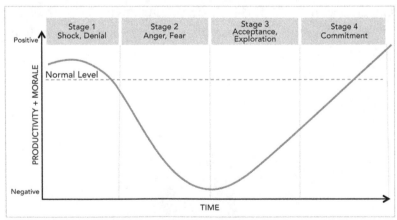

The change curve

transition and having patience and empathy as people move through the change curve.

At first, these emotions affect both productivity and morale but over time people tend to work through them until the change becomes the new normal. Here's the general pattern:

- **Stage 1: Change is announced, disrupting the status quo.** This might result in feelings of shock and denial. Employees tend to question the change or even ignore it and not take it that seriously. You might hear people say things like, "I can't believe they're doing this," "They'll never go through with it," and ask questions like, "How will this impact me?"

- **Stage 2: Change is met with anger and resistance.** In this phase, people realize that the change is not going away and they can get angry about it. Comments here might be, "This isn't a good plan and it won't work," or "Why are they doing this to us?" "It's unfair!" and "I don't like it."

- **Stage 3: Reluctant acceptance sets in.** At the bottom of the curve, people start to accept that they cannot avoid the change. You are likely to hear comments like, "It seems like this happening so I better get on board." At this point, you might notice people trying to negotiate a compromise that makes the change more favorable. They might make suggestions like, "How about if we just do this instead?"

- **Stage 4: Change is embraced with commitment.** People continue to move forward with the change, understanding what is needed and getting involved with the change. When you see evidence of hope and engagement, and hear things like, "I think this just might work," people have begun embracing the change. Because people are now on board, they get creative, often offering suggestions for how the change could be improved. And they might even become impatient, wanting the rollout even faster now that they feel ready. This commitment continues until the change is completed. At first there is excitement about the accomplishment, and you'll hear things like, "We did it!" And "How did we ever get by the old way?" Then things settle down and you are back to the status quo . . . until the next change initiative is announced.

The change curve provides a map through transition—and there is really no getting around it. Ignoring the messy feelings that change brings up won't make it go away and, in fact, will make things worse. Good leadership can shorten the length of time or lesson the height of the curve but it won't disappear completely because we are biologically wired to resist change. Leaders often need help preparing for the messiness of the process because they can become disheartened when they see how people react. In section IV, we'll explore skills that better equip leaders and managers to make the change and transition successful.

5. Houston, We Have a Problem

While the change curve model is useful, it doesn't entirely capture how change unfolds in the modern workplace.

First, it doesn't account for the four factors of disruption, time-to-acclimation, desire, and choice. As a result, the change curve does not address the full range of emotions that employees exhibit. For example, when change is announced employees might feel excitement and hope if it's something they want and they choose. If they don't want it or choose it, you might see frustration and resentment. And employees often experience stress, anxiety, confusion, and even depression as the change continues.

The first half of the curve is difficult because people naturally focus on the past and potential losses the change might bring. This is a biologically driven response (which we will explore in more depth in the next chapter on the brain science of change), but it's natural and normal and part of our species' survival instincts. This is not something that people can override or overcome. I often tell leaders, "They are not being difficult. They are being human."

When people hit the bottom of the curve, I have witnessed three types of resignation, which are not accounted for by the change curve. Employees might literally resign from the organization, quitting their jobs and thereby quitting the change, too. Or, leaders surprised by unexpected "drama" might decide to stop the change initiative rollout, quitting the change instead of having patience for the bottom of the

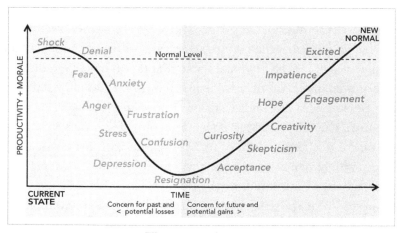

The emotions of transition

curve to turn. Or, the employees might make the psychological shift and resign themselves to the change, thus getting on board emotionally.

This psychological shift occurs because people are able to turn their focus to the future and look for potential gains. This is a pivotal, significant moment because it ushers in more positive feelings like curiosity, creativity, and excitement which carry through to the end of the change. Once you see acceptance, you will start to see a slow progression through more positive and forward-focused emotions, such as curiosity (with some healthy skepticism thrown in). People will also start asking a more questions. Leaders often find that they have to repeat information they have been saying for weeks once people start accepting the change, because instead of fighting against it they are actually listening.

Second, we aren't just going through one change at a time. Employees are often moving through several change curves simultaneously, perhaps at different stages on each one. You could be finishing up a change in your email system, for example, when you're told that you are getting a new supervisor. And a new policy might be implemented right in the middle of your move to a new work location or team. You don't always get the luxury of neatly arriving at the end of one change curve before you are launched onto one or several new ones. And what happens when you are starting to embrace one change, having feelings of hope and excitement, when a new change is announced that you feel resistance about? Do you backslide a little on the first change? My observations say yes, and yet current change models don't account for that.

Third, the change curve implies that all change is experienced the same by every member of the group. But we have already seen that key factors like disruption, acclimation, desire, and choice are not accounted for in this model. Doesn't it make sense that if you have high desire and choice for a change, you may have a different emotional reaction than another person who does not want or choose that change?

Fourth, the change curve doesn't account for a person's capacity to take on more change. Each of us has a bandwidth for change, which is how much change we can hold and still function effectively. If you just had a baby, I suspect your bandwidth is pretty full already and there's not a lot of room to take on more. Or if you are going through an acquisition, it might not be a good time to remodel your kitchen.

This happened to me: In the middle of a major kitchen remodel and dealing with an ailing parent, my company was purchased. If LinkedIn CEO Jeff Wiener had called me and asked if it was a good time for me, I would have told him that I'd prefer he waited a few months. My bandwidth for change was pretty maxed already, thank you very much.

But of course, that didn't happen, and I found myself dealing with so much change that if I had had a bandwidth meter, it would have blown out the top and exploded into a million little pieces. It was a difficult period, both physically and emotionally.

In this example, the acquisition, the kitchen, and my mom's health were all changes that were high disruption and high time-to-acclimation. But your bandwidth can also fill up with lots of small changes. How many yellow changes is too many? And what happens if you add a red or orange change to the mix?

In addition to bandwidth, most people have a preferred style for approaching and addressing change. According to research by Dr. Chris Musselwhite, people respond to change on a continuum, particularly in how they view the necessity for change and their own interest in participating.

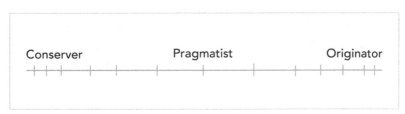

The change style continuum

On one end, you have the conservers, who are more cautious about change in general and tend to resist the unknown. When faced with change, they need a lot of information and a lot of time but are steady, reliable, and consistent. They prefer gradual change and they prefer to make small changes, retaining the current structure, rather than big shifts. Conservers ask good questions and keep people from making impulsive decisions, designing change that can gently transition the organization.

At the other end of the continuum are originators, who enjoy risk and are comfortable with change. As the creative thinkers or innovators in a group, they often propose change with a "Let's try it out" mindset.

They serve as the visionaries for change and often create new ways of doing business. However, they often need support thinking through the realities of implementation. They prefer change to be quick and radical and prefer to challenge the current structure.

In the middle, you have the pragmatists, who embrace change when they believe it is absolutely necessary. They are practical and reasonable but sometimes noncommittal. Because they sit in the middle of the conservers and originators, pragmatists often function as mediators between the other two, facilitating cooperation and communication. They prefer change to clearly serve a function and are willing to explore the current structure.

Most workplaces are filled with a fairly even mix of these change types, even at fast-growth tech start-ups, where you might expect to find a higher percentage of originators. (If you want to learn more, take Dr. Musselwhite's change-style-indicator assessment, found at DiscoveryLearning.com.)

The change curve assumes every person approaches change the same way when that is clearly not the case. Doesn't it make sense that originators might have a different psychological transition than conservers? I have certainly found this to be true.

All of these issues came together at a leading online travel booking website. The senior executives wanted to streamline their hiring practices so that all 100 of the recruiters were using the same strategies and processes. The VP of the recruiting function created a plan to shift everyone to a shared model. It was well designed and the company invested $100K in the process and related training. Once the change began rolling out, the recruiters experienced the typical emotions of the transition. They were adopting the new process and adjusting to it. However, the Chief People Officer was more cautious about change in general and was surprised to hear complaints.

While the VP explained that this was a normal part of the process, the CPO's discomfort grew with every grumble. Soon, 90 percent of the team turned the corner and were doing fine but one small group of less than ten people were struggling. They continued to complain regularly to the CPO, whose own discomfort for change and lack of understanding about transition, gave greater weight to their concerns. Eventually, the CPO pulled the change, claiming that it was not working. This cost the company not only their investment and hours of staff time but ultimately their competitive advantage.

6. The Rise of Change Fatigue

A new development in the modern workplace is change fatigue, which is lingering mental and physical tiredness associated with organizational change. It occurs when people just cannot keep up with the pace or volume of change coming their way. For small initiatives, the physical and psychological effort might be low but as more changes begin to overlap, a person's ability to successfully cope can become strained.

What are the signs of change fatigue in the workplace? From the front lines to the top executives, you might see several symptoms, including disengagement, exhaustion, absenteeism, confusion, conflict, and cynicism. You will also see a decline in performance across the group, even among your top performers.

Change Fatigue at Work	
Disengagement	People become apathetic and emotionally "check out"
Exhaustion	Lack of energy, staring into space, sleeping at work
Absenteeism	Leaving work early or taking more sick days
Confusion	Poor judgment and decision-making
Conflict	Tension and conflict between individuals and groups
Cynicism	Increased complaints, skepticism, and resistance

Symptoms of change fatigue

According to Dr. Janet Fitzell, change fatigue occurs when people feel both burdened by relentless change and powerless to stop it. She says it's brought about when the workplace seems like it has "become one unending change initiative with staff spending an increasing proportion of their time reacting to change instead of getting the job done."

In my work as a consultant, I have seen many examples of change fatigue. One multinational company was facing some financial struggles and started reorganizing. But they would barely complete one reorganization before they would start on the next. One function was especially impacted with employees being moved to new teams and supervisors every couple of months. I met several workers who had had six or seven new managers within one year! Naturally, they were not only fatigued, they were starting to become disengaged and the company saw more and more of their best employees leave.

This example specifically shows chronic change fatigue. Borrowing from medicine, chronic indicates an ongoing issue from which the patient does not improve. Those employees were experiencing a series of ongoing change initiatives that created chronic change fatigue because they could not get out of the cycle.

Compare that to acute change fatigue, which occurs suddenly and is intense but fairly short-lived. For example, when you start a new job and everything about your work environment has changed. You are meeting new people, getting to know your supervisor, and learning about your roles, responsibilities, and projects. You are finding your way around the buildings and perhaps even an entire campus of buildings. You're also learning how to ask for tech support, where to find the office supplies, how to use the copier, and perhaps a new email system or software. And if you are an executive, you are also learning about the business strategy, building rapport with the other executives and board members, and gaining information about all of the inner workings of your function, your organization, and the market.

Any new hire will tell you that those first few weeks are exhausting, both physically and emotionally. But fortunately, things get easier within six to eight weeks and you recover from the exhaustion and start to feel like yourself again.

Change fatigue is real and impacting organizations in every industry around the world. More and more studies are being done on change fatigue and its effect in the workplace. For example, in 2015 Ketchum, Inc., conducted a study of senior executives in seven countries. They found that nearly half (47 percent) of senior leaders felt change fatigue was highly prevalent in their organization. Tyler Durham, partner and president of Ketchum Change states that more leaders need to "recognize the exhausting effect that continuous change and volatility has on employees and how that exhaustion can lower employees' productivity, reduce their engagement and damage retention rates."

You can completely overwhelm a team with the right combination of yellow-, orange-, and red-zone changes strung together without sufficient recovery time in between. In fact, like the proverbial straw that broke the camel's back, even one or two ill-timed green changes can also do damage.

The human body cannot sustain unending change. It's just too exhausting, so people begin to make choices. They may first jump into change with enthusiasm, working hard to be successful. But when more and more changes come their way, they realize they cannot put that effort in each time. So they begin to disengage. By caring less about their job and their workplace, they don't feel so affected by it. But sadly, this means they are not bringing their passion or motivation to work either. Dr. Dawn-Marie Turner says that this is when companies begin to lose their competitive advantage, because they are losing the productivity and innovation that engaged employees bring.

The other thing that happens is that employees learn how to "play the change game" by looking like they are participating but actually expending as little energy as possible. Jeanie Duck, author of *The Change Monster*, calls them change survivors. This threatens the organization's success because leaders get a false sense that change is happening but don't see the results that it should be driving.

So, to properly interpret the change curve, keep in mind that it doesn't account for chronic or acute change fatigue. It assumes that every trip through the curve will unfold like all the others but when people are physically and emotionally exhausted, they are just not going to respond like employees who are not fatigued. As someone who studies the biology of work, I found that neuroscience shed light on understanding change, and more importantly how we better help people move through it.

Your Learning Journey

Let's use these concepts to assess your own experiences. I recommend first reflecting on a change that you have already completed and then looking ahead to what else is coming. Consider these questions:

- How would you rate the amount of disruption and time-to-acclimation? Which quadrant best represents the change?
- What is your motivation for the change? Did you want it and did you choose it? Which stick figure best represents your motivation (runner, walker, trudger, or resister)?
- How well did the change curve map to your experience? What did the different stages look like for you?
- What level was your change bandwidth at the time you were going through this change? Did you have plenty of room to accommodate it or were you feeling maxed out?
- Did you experience any change fatigue during this change? If so, which symptoms did you exhibit?

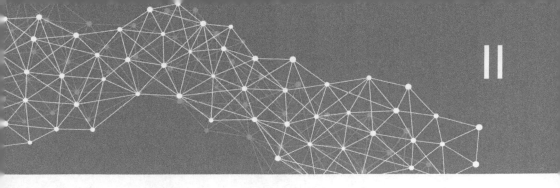

FEAR + FAILURE + FATIGUE:
THE BRAIN SCIENCE OF CHANGE

7. The Brain on Change

Exploring the neuroscience of change was a natural continuation of my research on the neuroscience of learning. (For more information on that subject, see my book titled *Wired to Grow: Harness the Power of Brain Science to Master Any Skill.*) Neuroscience is the study of how the central nervous system (brain and spinal cord) and the peripheral nervous system (all the other nerves throughout the body) work together to shape our thoughts, emotions, and behaviors.

Medical technology has allowed researchers from a wide range of disciplines like neurology, biology, and psychology, to name a few, to explore the inner workings of the human body in ways never seen before. In fact, as I read study after study in various academic journals, it seems clear we are experiencing a renaissance of sorts and coming to know ourselves on an entirely new level. We have lifted the hood, so to speak, and are finally getting a real grasp on how our engines run. I predict that the coming years will bring even more profound insights to the surface.

While I am not a neuroscientist (my doctorate is in Education, Leadership, and Organizations), I feel very fortunate that my years as faculty and dean at the University of California trained me to decipher empirical research—and more importantly—draw connections among seemingly unrelated studies. It always strikes me that, because of their deep specializations, most scientists are very isolated. So many of them are focused on a very tiny niche of research, often studying one brain function or even one specific brain structure. While brilliant in their specialty, they are not looking across a wide range of disciplines, nor are they applying their work to solving today's workplace problems.

As a working practitioner in the fields of learning and leadership development, I serve as a translator, harvesting the latest findings into actionable takeaways. In my cross-functional, multidisciplinary review of the literature, I have found certain aspects of the brain are vital for understanding how change impacts today's employees. The studies about these aspects immediately shined a light on some major gaps in how we understand change, which is directly related to why so many change initiatives are doomed.

Simply put, we are working against human biology at almost every turn. In the most basic terms, human are designed to do three things, in an ascending order:

1. **Survive:** Several aspects of our bodies and brains are built to scan for danger and help us survive a wide range of threats so that we can continue the species.

2. **Belong:** We are also wired to build connections with others in meaningful relationships and to form a sense of community. This aids our survival and also allows us to realize our core needs for camaraderie, friendship, and love.

3. **Become:** We are also designed to become our best selves— to seek to grow and improve so that we can realize our fullest potential. While this is a deep need, it can only occur once our survival and belonging needs are met.

This is my modified version of Dr. Abraham Maslow's famous Hierarchy of Needs, a model of human psychology and motivation that has stood the test of time. I find it interesting that even though the success of every organization depends on employees doing good work, and growing and improving over time, organizations often unintentionally threaten our need to survive and belong.

Change is often where and when that happens. As you will see, several aspects of the brain are dedicated to helping us survive, belong, and become. And change initiatives, when not handled correctly, can work against our biology and keep people from performing their best.

Many brain structures relate to change but I believe these four in particular are crucial to understand: the amygdala, the entorhinal cortex, the basal ganglia, and the habenula. I have been sharing the results of my research with executives around the world and every single one immediately saw the implications for their organizations and their people. And each one could identify several key issues that were not being addressed in their change plans.

In sections III and IV, I will show you how to weave these insights from neurosicence into a effective strategies you can implement.

Many of us remember the story of Chicken Little who, after being bonked on the head by a falling acorn, ran around crying, "The sky is falling! The sky is falling!"

This story actually demonstrates how one of our brain structures, the amygdala, functions. The amygdala is largely responsible for our survival. According to Dr. Anthony Wright, professor of neurobiology at the University of Texas Medical School, the amygdala is connected to all of the major sensory nerves (optical, aural, olfactory, etc.). It's designed to detect threats in our environment. When a potential threat arises, like the smell of fire smoke, seeing an attacker, or hearing a gunshot, the amygdala launches the fight-flight-freeze response.

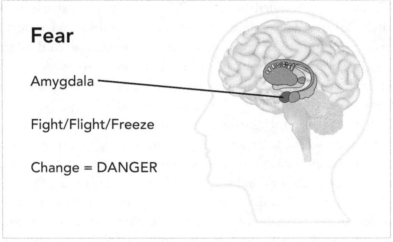

The amygdala and fear

Within 200 milliseconds, our body is flooded with adrenalin and cortisol, which rush through the body to prepare it to survive the impending danger. Increased blood flow helps muscles respond more quickly while increased blood coagulants can help us survive an injury. Lung capacity increases, the body releases natural painkillers, and the neocortex (the "thinking" brain) shuts down, taking away advanced logic and self-awareness.

Most of us have experienced this intense and powerful reaction, perhaps when another car has swerved near us or we have been attacked by an animal or a person. The emotional feeling of this response is first

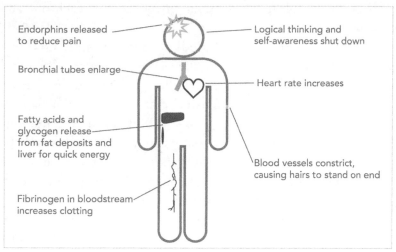

Impact of adrenalin and cortisol

fear often followed by anger, so it is no surprise that we see those emotions at the beginning of the change curve.

It is interesting to note that the amygdala is wired to detect *change*—any change, even the smallest, most miniscule changes. This is because our species was most likely to survive if we approached our environment with caution and suspicion. Noticing that a bush looked different today could be the difference between life and death, because there might be a lion or an enemy lurking behind it. While it may have been a group of fluffy bunnies, we were more likely to survive to tell the tale at the campfire when we assumed the worst.

From an evolutionary perspective, we who are alive now are descendants of the early humans who were most sensitive to change and most cautious in response to it. For a humorous depiction of this wiring, watch the animated movie *The Croods*. Nicolas Cage plays the patriarch whose motto is "Never not be afraid," and as a result his family survives while all their neighbors perish.

In today's modern world, our sensory nerves are constantly scanning our environment and when things are as expected, we feel calm. But when we detect change, we are wired to go on alert and assume the worst until proven otherwise.

In fact, our need to survive is so strong that others who have gone into fear easily influence us. The way Chicken Little's fear convinces her friends Henny Penny and Ducky Lucky that the sky is falling. When they ask her how she knows, she says, "Because it landed on my head," which is good enough to set off their amygdalas too, each one adding to the collective hysteria.

I have witnessed this in all kinds of organizations. One or two people can influence the rest of the group, spreading "doom and gloom" perspectives and amping up the group's fear and distress. Leaders are often surprised and frustrated at how easily this happens.

That's why it's important to assess how disruptive the change might be and how people will respond given their desire for and choice of the change. If you have a couple of trudgers or resisters in the midst of a group who is walking toward the change, they may not have much impact unless they are highly influential to the others.

It's also important to be transparent and share as much information as you can as early as possible. Psychologists have long known that in the absence of information, the brain fills in the blanks—but it doesn't just fill in any story. According to psychologist Dr. Janice Rudestam, the brain fills in the *worst-case scenario*.

This is how rumors of budget cuts and layoffs can run rampant in an organization. Employees usually sense that something is afoot and begin filling in the blanks with horrible possibilities. Again, this is part of our biological wiring—we are more likely to survive if we plan for the worst instead of hoping for the best. When people get anxious and start worrying about things that are not really an issue, they are not being difficult, they are being human. But they can only really shift perspective with information delivered by a trusted person.

Leaders and managers can address this by driving a clear and consistent narrative about the why and how of the change. I'll get more into the details in future chapters but for now, just understand that fear and anxiety are a big part of how humans respond to change. It's just the truth of our biology.

As you may have already guessed, the amygdala is responsible for the first half of the change curve. All those negative emotions are swirling around and people have lost their logical analysis and self-awareness, which would help them make better choices. Most of us have learned to temper the raw intensity of the amygdala's fight-flight-freeze response, however. Rarely does it look like punching someone or running away. Instead, the modern fight response includes criticism, contempt, sarcasm, teasing, and shaming, in addition to aggression. And even aggression is likely to be contained to raising the voice, pounding a hand on a table, or slamming a door.

Likewise, the modern flight-freeze response is more often going to look like people getting quiet or withdrawn, or they may engage in defensiveness, stonewalling, making excuses, or blaming others. These are all attempts to shift attention to others.

The Story of Chicken Little

Chicken Little likes to walk in the woods. She likes to look at the trees. She likes to smell the flowers. She likes to listen to the birds singing.

One day while she is walking an acorn falls from a tree, and hits the top of her little head.

"My, oh, my, the sky is falling! I must run and tell the lion about it," says Chicken Little and begins to run. She runs and runs. By and by she meets the hen.

"Where are you going?" asks the hen.

"Oh, Henny Penny, the sky is falling and I am going to the lion to tell him about it."

"How do you know?" asks Henny Penny.

"It hit me on the head, so I know it must be so," says Chicken Little.

"Let me go with you!" says Henny Penny. "Run, run!"

So the two run and run until they meet Ducky Lucky.

"The sky is falling," says Henny Penny. "We are going to the lion to tell him about it."

"How do you know that?" asks Ducky Lucky.

"It hit Chicken Little on the head," says Henny Penny.

"May I come with you?" asks Ducky Lucky.

"Come," says Henny Penny.

So all three of them run on and on until they meet Foxey Loxey.

"Where are you going?" asks Foxey Loxey.

"The sky is falling and we are going to the lion to tell him about it," says Ducky Lucky.

"Do you know where he lives?" asks the fox.

"I don't," says Chicken Little.

"I don't," says Henny Penny.

"I don't," says Ducky Lucky.

"I do," says Foxey Loxey. "Come with me. I'll show you the way."

He walks on and on until he comes to his den.

"Come right in," says Foxey Loxey.

They all go in, but they never, never come out again.

As people engage in these challenging behaviors, like criticism and blame, they can affect each other so that team dynamics can become strained or harmed. People are strained and operating from a state of fear that can easily escalate. No wonder leaders are likely to see a decline in productivity and morale!

Like all good children's stories, Chicken Little has a message. As Chicken Little, Henny Penny, and Ducky Lucky continue their journey, they run into Foxey Loxey, who sees that they are distraught and hyped up on adrenalin. Sensing an opportunity, he takes advantage of their emotional state, offering to "help" but leading them to his den, where they are never seen again.

As this fable accurately depicts, heightened states of fear and anxiety can distract us, causing us to make unwise choices. While it's unlikely that we'll become someone's dinner, losing our self-awareness and logical analysis make us prone to injuries and accidents as well as producing defective or low quality work.

Part of leading change successfully is understanding and being prepared for the powerful fear response. When leaders and managers are ready for the side effects of the amygdala, they are much more likely to help their people through the change curve effectively and increase the likelihood of success for the change initiative.

In summary, if the amygdala could talk during change, it would say, "I'm freaking out!"

9. Entorhinal Cortex: Our Personal GPS

As I explored the brain science of change, the Nobel Prize–winning work of Drs. May-Britt and Edvard Moser stood out as having important implications. They co-lead the Center for the Biology of Memory at the Norwegian University of Science and Technology and the Kavli Institute for Systems Neuroscience. The Mosers discovered that our brain has an internal geographical positioning system (GPS) that helps us navigate our way through physical space. Their fascinating research shows that the entorhinal cortex, which sits within the hippocampus, is the brain structure responsible for our GPS capabilities. It contains a spherical cluster of cells that actually make maps of our physical surroundings and helps us successfully navigate our way through them.

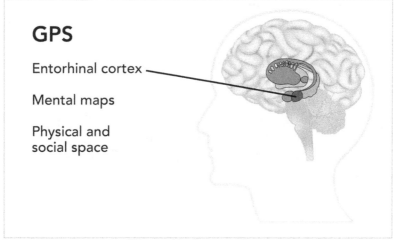

The entorhinal cortex and maps

The Mosers attached computer monitors to rats that showed the activity of the entorhinal cortex on a screen, creating a visual representation. And what they saw was mind-blowing: the sphere of cells was organized in a grid-like pattern, with the cells activating in a way that created a visual map. In other words, they could see the cells light up, one by one, as the rat walked around, showing accurate direction, distance, and even speed or pace. The cells even indicated a boundary when the rat encountered a wall. As the rat moved, the cells literally created an accurate map of the space—in all three dimensions. If that same rat was placed in a new location, the entorhinal cortex would build a new map. And if the rat was returned to the previous location, the existing map was "loaded," allowing the rat to quickly find its way around. If something in the environment had shifted, the mental map was revised.

This internal GPS system is vital to the survival of every species. It allows us to find our way back to sources of food, water, and shelter, and it reduces the mental and physical energy of having to figure it out each time.

We all have thousands of maps in our brains of various places we have lived and worked. Have you ever visited a neighborhood or school from your childhood? Or an old workplace? Your brain loaded up that old map, allowing you to find things you hadn't seen in years. And you probably could clearly see where things were different ("Huh, this is where the meeting room used to be"), evidence that your entorhinal cortex was updating your map.

These mental maps not only help us survive, they can create a sense of familiarity and belonging, something that we are biologically wired to seek. And some companies are able to harness this into long-term customer loyalty. For example, Waterfall Resort Alaska provides high-end sport-fishing adventures every summer. Started over 100 years ago, the lodge now regularly hosts guests who are the grandchildren of their original clients. These families make it a tradition to come back year after year because of their fond memories for both the location and the quality experience the staff provides.

Many of today's large hotel and resort chains also leverage our mental maps by creating consistent experiences down to the room layout, furnishings, and bedding. These executives know that traveling is stressful and many customers prefer to arrive at a place that feels familiar. By having a mental map that applies to multiple locations, it saves the traveler both physical and emotional energy.

Interestingly, the Mosers' research is shedding light on why Alzheimer's patients become disoriented. It turns out that this cluster of grid cells gets damaged early in the course of the disease, thus disabling their mental maps of the places they should know. Even though they are navigating places they have been hundreds of times before, the internal map has disappeared and along with it, their recognition of a place as familiar.

GPS and Change

What does this mean for change in today's workplace? Many changes may affect people's mental maps of their physical workplaces. We might move the location of an employee's workstation or office, or we might move certain services or resources, like where food can be found or the location of the tech support team. In the case of a relocation or acquisition, every single aspect of the work environment might be disrupted and replaced with something new and unfamiliar. This is also true for every employee who is starting a new job. We have to build completely new mental maps of our work locations including how to get there, where we do our work, where colleagues sit, as well as resources like bathrooms, the copier, kitchen, and coffee. And if we moved our home to a new neighborhood for that job, then we must also build new mental maps of grocery stores, medical offices, restaurants, etc.

Fortunately, the brain can and will build new mental maps. But this process takes some time and energy as the person navigates the new space. That's part of the reason we feel mental and physical fatigue when we start something new or go through a big change—the map-making part of our brain is doing some heavy lifting. And we are not just making maps of the physical space, but the social space too.

Social GPS

The Mosers are not the only researchers exploring the entorhinal cortex and the hippocampus it resides within. Research out of New York shows that these structures are also involved with creating social maps of people and relationships. Dr. Rita Tavares, from the Schiller Laboratory of Affective Neuroscience at the Icahn School of Medicine at Mount Sinai, states, "Beyond framing physical locations, the hippocampus computes a more general, inclusive, abstract, and multidimensional social map."

As we enter new social spaces, like a workplace or neighborhood, our brain scans for information and is actually able to map relationships based on power (which includes hierarchy, dominance, competence) as well as affinity (trustworthiness, love, intimacy). Functional neuroimaging scanners (fMRI) show that the hippocampus is activated when we are navigating new social settings, proof that the mapping function is taking place.

As with physical space, social space is often affected by workplace change. An employee will unconsciously reassess and revise their current social maps when they get a new manager or leader as well as when coworkers and team members change. And if they are starting a brand new job or new location, they will have to build entirely new social maps of all of the coworkers and colleagues across the organization with whom they interact.

This is why the hiring and onboarding experience is so important. We begin building our social maps during the application and interview process and our feelings about the people we meet greatly influence our decisions to accept jobs. One tech giant in Silicon Valley was losing a lot of great candidates to their competitors. A deeper analysis discovered that many of the hiring managers were using a "trial by fire" philosophy during interviews, while the competitors were using a "welcome to our family" approach.

Our social networks matter because we are wired to seek safety and belonging. During change, people fear the loss of those connections. We spend quite a bit of time developing our professional and social networks, building trust and rapport over time through many interactions. Many workplace initiatives erase the results of that effort, forcing us to start over.

Now, our brains are made to do this, so we will make new social maps and will eventually build trust and rapport, but, again, it takes time and energy. This contributes to the very real issue of change fatigue. And if an employee is experiencing a series of changes over a short period of time (for example, several moves of their workstation), the exhaustion and fatigue may become chronic, driving employee disengagement and attrition.

It's vital that leaders consider the physical space and social network implications for change iniatives. When impacted by change, the phrase for the entorhinal cortex would be, "I'm lost."

10. Basal Ganglia: Our Habit Factory

Another brain structure involved with any change we experience is the basal ganglia, which is responsible for taking behaviors we do frequently and turning them into habits. You constantly experience the benefits of your basal ganglia. When you learn something new, like how to use your smartphone or a piece of software, it is the basal ganglia that changes the activity from something challenging that requires a lot of concentration to something easy that you don't even have to think about.

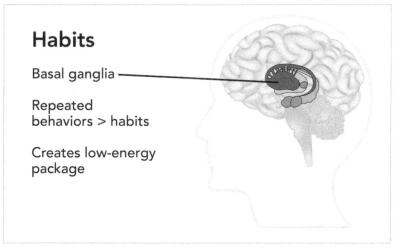

The basal ganglia and habits

Think about when you learned how to drive or ride a bike, to cook or bake, to pay bills and manage your finances. All of these activities took focus and concentration as you learned them but after enough successful repetitions, you probably do them on autopilot.

In work settings, some examples of your habits include how you manage your time, how you approach meetings, how you complete a project, and how you lead and manager others.

Researchers at the Brain and Cognitive Sciences department at the Massachusetts Institute of Technology discovered that the basal ganglia's purpose is to save brain energy, something that scientists can measure by the amount of glucose being used in the brain. Study after study shows that the more we do something, the less cognitive energy it takes and the basal ganglia is the structure that makes this happen.

Consider how you currently log in to your computer or how you get to work. When you first started, you had to think about it. As the basal ganglia turns that routine into a habit, it frees up our brain and allows us to spend mental energy on other important tasks like logical analysis and learning new things.

Essentially, the basal ganglia turns repeated behaviors into habit loops. A habit loop has three parts:

- **Cue:** For example, getting in your car is the cue, or trigger, to begin the behavior of driving. Or walking in to your kitchen at night is the cue to begin cooking dinner.

- **Routine:** The behavior itself. It's the act of driving: looking in mirrors, turning the steering wheel, stepping on the brake; or of chopping onions, pulling out a skillet, turning on the burner.

- **Reward:** The reward we get for completing the routine. With driving it's getting to our destination and for cooking, it's getting both the nourishment and taste of food.

Scientists have discovered that rewards are most effective when delivered immediately after completing a routine, like when we drive or cook. They get less effective the longer we have to wait after engaging in a behavior. This is why so many people struggle with getting in shape, eating healthfully, or quitting smoking. The new rewards of toned muscles, smaller clothes, or better blood pressure will be realized too far into the future, through incremental and often invisible shifts. From the brain's perspective, that's not very compelling, especially when eating healthy or working out might actually seem punishing at first.

The other interesting thing about rewards is that you don't have to use them forever, only until the habit loop is formed. Charles Duhigg, in his book *The Power of Habit*, shares one study of a group of people who wanted to exercise more. Split into two groups, both had the same cue (when you wake up) and routine (go for a run). But Group A was given a reward when they returned, a small piece of chocolate. They didn't do this forever; only until the habit was well formed. But the results were clear. Group A formed the habit and participants maintained the habit for far longer than those in Group B.

This got me thinking about how rarely we praise or reward people at work. Sure, you might get an annual performance review but it's likely to be a mix of praise and areas for improvement. And while it may come with a bonus, it's too removed from the completion of an actual routine to create a meaningful link in the brain.

Another key factor is that habits are built through repetition. As you do the behavior over and over again, you build up the neural pathway to the point that scientists can see the neurons getting thicker with use. In fact, studies show that it takes 40 to 50 repetitions, on average, to establish a new habit. It's through repetition that the basal ganglia shifts the routine to be an automatic response.

If you need anymore convincing about the importance of habits at work, consider the story of Rick Rescorla, a security guard who worked for Morgan Stanley at the World Trade Center in New York. After the WTC was bombed in 1993, Rescorla was upset about how disorganized the evacutation had been and he also worried that future attacks were likely given the iconic nature of the buildings. As a result, he insisted that all 2,700 employees, including senior executives, regularly practice evacuating from their offices, which occupied twenty two floors of the South Tower. He would grab a bullhorn, and despite complaints from employees who wanted to focus on work, he would have them practice taking the stairs down.

He didn't just do this once or twice. He made them practice *every three months*. So when the unthinkable happened on September 11, 2001, and the first plane hit the North Tower, the 2,687 employees who were at work that day knew exactly what to do. Despite the terror and confusion, their practice kicked in and they all got out safely. Those survivors credit Rescorla with saving their lives.

Habits and Change

Obviously, when we initiate change, we are likely to impact the well-developed habit loops that people already have in place. In all my years of consulting, I cannot think of a single change initiative that didn't require people to shift their behaviors in some profound way. Whether it's moving to a different email system, selling or marketing to a new type of client, or creating an innovative product, change involves building new habits and, worse, leaving comfortable old habits that are easy to do and have predictable rewards.

Change requires people to focus and concentrate until they sufficiently learn the new cues and the new routines, which as we've seen takes time and a lot of energy and can lead to change fatigue. In addition, we often expect people to build a new habit without offering compelling rewards for doing so. In fact, the new way usually (at least at first) takes more time and energy than the old way, which can seem more like a punishment to the brain. Is anyone really surprised, then, that so many change initiatives fail?

Let's take a common and costly example. Many companies have to make changes that affect their sales team, like shifting software or changing the way a product is marketed. Like any team, these changes will require new habits, which takes time and energy to develop. And the longer those new habits take to build, the more likely the company will see a dip in its own profit. This kind of impact may impact all the teams—engineering, HR, marketing—but for the sales teams, the potential punishment is even worse. Every minute of decreased productivity may also decrease their quota-based pay. In other words, they are likely to get paid less during the transition even while doing the same amount, or even more, work. Yikes—talk about a punishment!

For everyone, concerns about salary are likely to trigger the amygdala because money is key to our survival in modern times. We can't just go out and build a new shelter or hunt/forage for our dinner. Our paychecks allow us access to shelter, food, and water, so affecting an employee's ability to make money is not only a punishment, it's highly threatening to survival.

You would think that companies would help sales teams make the transition as quickly as possible by investing in quality training and coaching, things that help people build new habits and adjust to change. But the truth is that rarely happens. They may hold some training that provides information about the change, but not training that works with the brain to move people through the transition and develop the right habits quickly.

We'll explore what kinds of rewards matter and to how to create effective training in future chapters but suffice it to say that the basal ganglia plays a major role in successful change, and ignoring how it works contributes to the dismal success we see with change initiatives.

During change, the basal ganglia would say, "I don't know what to do."

11. Habenula: Our Failure-Avoidance Center

Only recently has imaging technology allowed scientists to truly see and study the habenula, which is located deep in the center of our brain, near the thalamus. The habenula is responsible for decision-making and actions. It does this by creating chemical guardrails that moderate our behavior.

Our brain naturally releases dopamine and serotonin, the "feel-good" chemicals, when we do something right. This is part of the brain's reward system. You probably feel it when you accomplish a task or receive praise for a job well done. However, when we make a poor choice that does not lead to a reward, the habenula restricts the flow of those chemicals, cutting off the drip so to speak, making us feel bad.

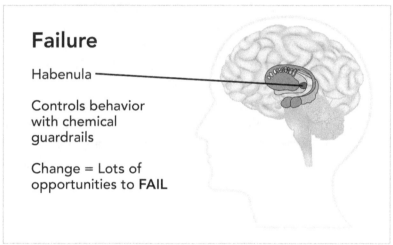

The habenula and failure

The habenula's role is quite important to the survival of our species. In our hunter-gatherer days, it would help us repeat good choices like going back to the trail that led to a food source (reward), and making us uncomfortable about the trail that didn't have food. It's almost like a chemical game of "warmer/colder" or the reins on a horse, guiding us toward and away from good choices.

In our modern world, it still helps us repeat successful behaviors like returning to a restaurant where we had a good meal or approaching a work project in a similar way to a previous one that turned out well.

Scientists have also discovered that the habenula is hyperactive in people with severe depression, which over-restricts serotonin and dopamine so that they feel bad all the time. In addition, the habenula plays a crucial role in regulating sleep patterns, including rapid eye movement (REM) and circadian rhythms.

But the habenula does more than help us repeat behaviors that will bring rewards. It also helps us avoid punishment. According to Dr. Okihide Hikosaka, at the National Institutes of Health Laboratory of Sensorimotor Research, "Failing to obtain a reward is disappointing and disheartening, but to be punished may be worse." Studies have shown that the habenula is also very active when we approach a task where we have received a punishment. In fact, it suppresses not only our motivation but also our physical body movements. In other words, we don't want to do the behavior, but it's more difficult to make our body do the behavior as well. Talk about a double whammy! You can't get excited to do it but even if you managed to psych yourself up, your body won't get on board. If you ever find yourself thinking, *I just can't seem to make myself do it*, you're probably caught in this cycle.

This whole process can be exacerbated by stress. When a person is under sustained, uncontrollable stress, the body responds by inducing various immune responses such as increasing inflammatory chemicals. The body is essentially treating the stress as a physical threat and responding like it would to bacteria or a virus, like the flu, including suppressing motivation and motor movements. In other words, you feel tired all the time and have little energy or desire to get things done.

When we're physically sick, this response helps us to get better. It essentially forces us to rest, saving our energy so our immune system can overcome the source of the illness and return us to health. But in situations of sustained stress, it creates depression and lethargy that can go on and on.

When stress and the habenula's natural function to avoid failure come together, you can unintentionally create "learned helplessness," a concept first identified by psychologist Dr. Martin Seligman, who went on to found the Positive Psychology movement. He had been conducting experiments with dogs that were being classically conditioned by receiving a mild shock, a form of punishment, when they heard a bell. Once that conditioning was in place, he put the dogs in a room where they had freedom to move away from the source of the shock. But guess what happened? They lay down and gave up.

Seligman's research, and many subsequent studies, have shown that if we have enough negative experiences we become conditioned to expect failure and we just give up and stop trying—and here is the most important part—even when things have changed! In other words, we reach a point where we just can't motivate ourselves emotionally or physically to try anymore.

Many psychologists believe that learned helplessness is at play in all kinds of situations: people who cannot leave an abusive situation, students who no longer try to succeed in a subject like math, people with health problems who continue to make the same unhealthy choices. In the work setting, learned helplessness can affect people and teams. If conditions have been bad enough for long enough, change won't necessarily overcome the learned helplessness. I have seen numerous situations where a solution has been implemented, like a poor leader is replaced or more resources are provided, and the people involved don't shift to a healthier state. Clearly, this can be very confusing to leaders.

The habenula's function around failure can also be seen in a very common workplace process: the performance review. Dr. Markus Ullsperger and Dr. Yves von Cramon at the Max Planck Institute for Human Cognitive and Brain Sciences used MRI machines to view brain activity as people received feedback about their performance. When people were given negative feedback, a form of punishment, their habenulas were highly activated, creating another feel-bad experience.

No wonder employees and managers alike have come to dread the annual review process. The very process that is supposed to help people improve their performance becomes fraught with negative feelings. Performance reviews are known to kick off the amygdala's fear response as well. Oh, the irony.

Failure and Change

Understandably, the habenula is going to activate during change initiatives because change creates so many opportunities to fail. Think about all the potential "failures" for employees:
- Missing a milestone or deadline of the change plan
- Misreading new social dynamics in a way that affects a relationship
- Being tired and making mistakes in everyday tasks
- Having an emotional reaction that bothers others
- Not developing the new habits/behaviors fast enough
- Losing a job due to redundancy or poor performance

For the leaders and managers, the list includes those above as well as these additional opportunities for failure:

- Designing an ineffective change
- Miscalculating the change's costs or benefits
- Designing an ineffective change plan
- Undercommunicating or miscommunicating the change plan
- Miscalculating followers' change bandwidth
- Launching too many changes simultaneously or in succession
- Not allowing sufficient time for people to move through the change plan and the change curve
- Not preparing for the emotions of the change curve
- Not designing the right behaviors to support the change
- Not providing training that develops the right habits
- Not offering compelling rewards to motivate new behaviors and habits

Change brings opportunities to fail, and when we do, our brains and our bodies become more and more resistant to embracing future changes. I think it's likely that many of those initial negative emotions on the change curve are remnants of past failure.

Failure as an adult can also trigger some of our most painful memories of childhood failure and shame. As Dr. Brené Brown, an internationally recognized scholar on the effects of shame describes in her book *Daring Greatly*, "childhood experiences of shame change who we are, how we think about ourselves, and our sense of self-worth." Most often, children are shamed by parents and teachers when they make mistakes at home and at school.

Sadly, shaming doesn't stop when we grow up. I have seen managers attempt to "motivate" their teams by publicly shaming employees. And coworkers may use shaming as a defensive technique when their amygdala is activated. Dr. Brown's research goes on to show the profound and negative impacts of shaming in the workplace and how it harms creativity, innovation, collaboration, and productivity. If failure is combined with shame, the negative feelings will completely suppress both the motivation and willingness to try again.

I believe our previous lack of understanding about the habenula has contributed to the high failure rate of change initiatives. During change, the habenula's phrase would be, "I can't mess up."

12. The Dangerous Biological Cocktail

All four of these brain structures are individually powerful but change creates a situation where they are all likely to be activated simultaneously. The resulting biological cocktail is not easily overcome through sheer will power or inspirational leadership or training.

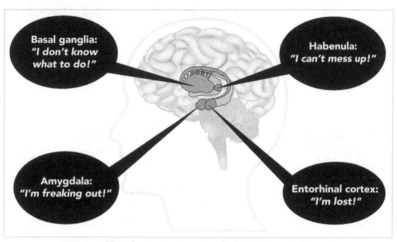

Four brain structures involved with change

Let's take a look at three very common change initiatives and how the brain plays its part. These are summaries of real situations from well-known organizations.

Scenario 1: A Thousand Small Changes

It's the second quarter and the sales team is working on its regular quarterly sales goals. It's business as usual and the team is rolling along. However, several departments have been working independently on changes that will be rolled out in Q2, each carefully designed for the lowest-possible impact on employees.

The IT department is rolling out a conversion to a different email and calendar system. While it's implemented over the weekend, it takes several weeks for people to develop the habits (basal ganglia) of the new system.

In the meantime, Facilities is continuing its yearlong rollout of new cubicles and the sales building is scheduled in Q2. While people will stay in the same building, their cubicle location and size will change as well as how much storage room they have. While the change occurs over the weekend, it still affects both habits (basal ganglia) and GPS (entorhinal cortex).

During the same quarter, Finance rolls out a new travel policy that affects meal allotments (decreased) and how receipts can be submitted for reimbursement. Several of the sales team travel to trade shows and must attend training on the new method. This change affects well-grooved habits (basal ganglia) and creates opportunities to fail (habenula).

The sales team, of course, experiences both change fatigue and stress as they worry that they won't hit their sales targets, affecting their income (amygdala, habenula).

Scenario 2: A Bunch of Medium and Large Changes

A competitor is gaining ground on market share and the executives are trying to correct the downward turn in revenue. Marketing and sales team leaders have been replaced, with the expectation that new leadership will help fix things. As a result, many employees are assigned to new managers. This disruptive change causes some anxiety (amygdala), shifts in social networks (entorhinal cortex), habits of workflow (basal ganglia), and performance (habenula).

In addition, the product team has been charged with completely redesigning the product while being reorganized into cross-functional teams. This changes supervisor relationships (entorhinal cortex), and requires embracing new ways of working (basal ganglia, habenula).

As expected, it takes time for the respective teams to adjust to these significant changes, which affects their overall performance. When the performance review process arrives, most of the affected employees receive a "meets expectations" evaluation, which impacts potential salary increases and bonuses (amygdala and habenula).

Scenario 3: A Huge, Career-Altering Change

A large global corporation purchases a small company and implements a thoughtful and robust transition plan. During the announcement, employees are both worried and excited (amygdala). During the first quarter, many redundant employees are let go and job titles are downgraded to match the acquiring company's system. Teams are split up and absorbed into different functions of the larger company, changing networks, locations, and reporting relationships (amygdala, entorhinal cortex, basal ganglia).

During the second quarter, many systems and processes shift over to those used by the purchasing company. IT switches employee computers, software, and phone systems. HR migrates to different payroll and time-tracking vendors. And Finance implements several new policies and procedures for purchasing, reimbursements, and travel. Most top-line managers are replaced with managers from the purchasing company, which changes reporting relationships and work expectations (amydgala, entorhinal cortex, basal ganglia, habenula).

By the third quarter, the purchasing company has rebranded everything with their logo, values, mission, etc., replacing coffee mugs, letterhead, and signage, and painting walls with approved brand colors (basal ganglia, entorhinal cortex).

As we consider how all of these brain structures work together, you can begin to see why, over time, people can become less flexible and adaptable to change and, worse, more anxious and worried about it. Our brains can begin to associate "change" of any kind with fear, failure, and fatigue so that it becomes a vicious cycle that impacts both employees and leaders. You could be rolling out the best-designed and most effective change your organization has ever seen, but its success depends on what else is happening or has happened in the past.

Given all this, it's actually surprising that 30 percent to 50 percent of change initiatives succeed, especially when we consider the real and compelling evidence that our brains are wired to resist change. But here's the good news: We can use the way the brain works to our advantage. The same structures that create challenges can be harnessed to create success, as we'll explore in the next section.

Your Learning Journey

Think about a few changes in your life and consider which aspects of the brain are likely to be involved.

1. Amygdala (Fear)
   - Is the change sudden or announced in a dramatic way?
   - Does it cause you feelings of anxiety or worry?
   - Is any aspect obviously threatening to you?
   - What can you do to make yourself feel safer?

2. Entorhinal cortex (GPS: physical space and social relationships)
   - Will the change affect your physical workspace or location?
   - Does it impact relationships or social dynamics?
   - Will it affect your home or neighborhood?
   - What can you do to quickly build new physical and social maps?

3. Basal ganglia (Habits)
   - To implement the change, what new behaviors will you need to develop?
   - Do you currently have a habit in place? If so, identify the cue, routine, and reward.
   - For new behaviors, consider what the cue, routines, and rewards could or should be.
   - Will training be provided to help you develop the new habit?
   - How can you quickly get to 40–50 repetitions?

4. Habenula (Failure)
   - What opportunities to fail exist with this change?
   - Have you previously failed on a similar change? If so, what were the consequences to you?
   - How does your organization view failure? In that culture or environment, is it okay to take risks? What happens when people make mistakes?
   - How can you create an experience that makes learning positive?

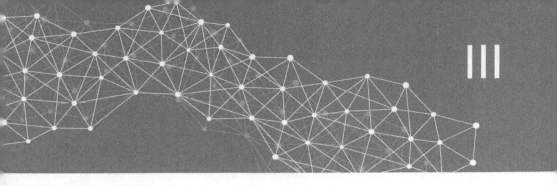

A NEW MODEL FOR CHANGE +
TRANSITION: THE CHANGE JOURNEY

13. The Change Journey Model.
Mountains Instead of Valleys

From my research, it became clear to me that we needed a new model of understanding change that incorporated the various issues:
- The four factors: disruption, acclimation, desire, and choice
- The change curve
- Individual bandwidth
- Change fatigue
- The neuroscience of how the four brain structures respond to change (amygdala, entorhinal cortex, basal ganglia, habenula)

A comprehensive model would ideally be both diagnostic and predictive, helping distinguish between different kinds of changes and also clarifying which leadership skills are needed to successfully help people move through them.

I built this Change Journey model to synthesize all the elements and studies we reviewed in previous chapters so that it accounts for the psychology and biology of the transition. You'll notice that my model keeps the change curve but makes three key shifts: First, I have flipped the curve upside down so that instead of looking like a descent into a valley, it shows the ascent up a mountain so its depiction better represents the physical and emotional effort that occurs when first experiencing change.

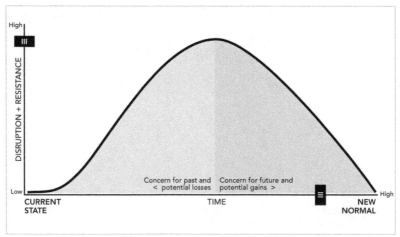

Presenting the Change Journey model

Second, the vertical axis has now switched from being a measure of productivity and morale to a measure of disruption and resistance, from low to high.

Third, in addition to integrating knowledge from several different tools, the Change Journey model is designed to be interactive, allowing you to adjust the axes (depicted as movable levers) to gain a clearer picture of how the change will be perceived and experienced by employees.

You can now dial along the vertical axis to indicate how disruptive the change is predicted to be. The more disruptive a change, the more resistance you are likely to get, and the higher the mountain, if you will, is likely to be.

The horizontal axis of time is something you can adjust as well to reflect whether a change will occur over a short (days to weeks), medium (weeks to months), or long (months to years) amount of time.

By sliding the levers, so to speak, you can more accurately diagram the disruption and acclimation elements that drive so much of the emotional transition process.

You can now see that people typically move through four distinct types of change journeys that map to the red, orange, yellow, and green zones we discussed in chapter 3:
- The long, intense climb (red)
- The quick hike up a steep hill (orange)
- The long, steady trek (yellow)
- The pebble on the trail (green)

These change journeys are very different from each other, eliciting different emotions and reactions. Unlike the change curve, this model shows variations in emotional responses for each of the major change journeys.

Finally, this model also allows you to estimate employee desire and choice, again allowing up to four options that represent their motivation. And you can also account for bandwidth and fatigue. Employees are considered travelers that leaders assist through the journey.

In this section, we'll take a closer look at each element and how you can use it to better predict and lead change.

1. The Long, Intense Climb

This hardest of the journeys most closely maps to the original change curve in terms of employee emotions. It represents a "red zone" change with high disruption and high time-to-acclimation.

Because that change will be highly disruptive, it will drive more resistance so you will see the full range of challenging emotions plus the initial focus on the past and potential losses. At the peak, you have resignation, which still implies people quitting, getting on board, or leaders calling it off. If we are keeping with our mountain motif, employees would get off the top of the mountain via helicopter or gondola.

Once people make the transition of looking toward the future and potential gains, emotions become more positive and the descent contributes to more momentum and less effort.

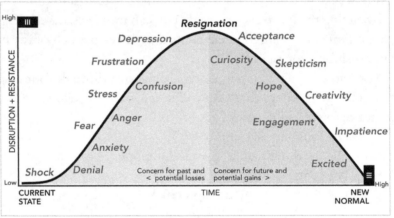

The "long, intense climb" journey

2. The Quick Hike Up a Steep Hill

This type of change still has a high amount of disruption but it will be over fairly quickly. It will require a burst of effort and focus, thus generating more resistance, especially if employees are already busy.

The sheer speed of the journey means you experience a flurry of intense emotions including resentment, overwhelm, and annoyance. But the speed also means that you can get to the peak of resignation and acceptance quicker.

On the backside of the peak, employees are likely to still feel overwhelm and will probably experience relief at the end.

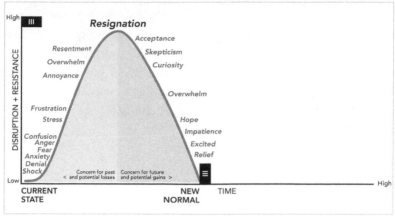

The "quick hike up a steep hill" journey

3. The Long, Steady Trek

This type of change does not create much disruption but will unfold over a long period of time, thus requiring stamina. Because disruption is low, employees are likely to experience far fewer negative emotions, with the worst being more about the length of the journey. Because of the amount of time, employees will likely still focus on the past and losses first but will eventually turn toward the future.

Notice that boredom is a new emotion in this model and will need to be addressed as people can tire of the long timeframe. At the end of this journey, employees are likely to feel both impatient and relieved.

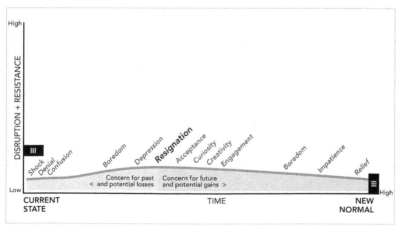

The "long, steady trek" journey

4. The Pebble on the Trail

Because it does not create disruption and is over so quickly, a pebble on the trail creates no emotional aspects to address nor does the focus on past losses or future gains come in to play. This is almost a non-event and practically invisible in the big scheme of things, unless it's added on top of several other difficult changes.

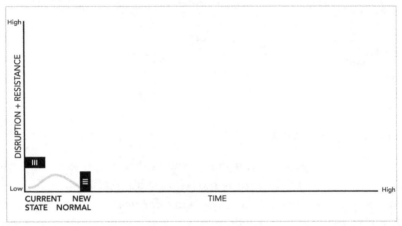

The "pebble on the trail" journey

By making this Change Journey model adjustable based on disruption and time-to-acclimation, we can now distinguish between different types of changes and you can get a much clearer picture of what the change journey is going to look like. This can provide valuable guidance about the skills that leaders and managers will need to move people through that change journey.

This model is actually an interactive tool you can use to assess and predict change. See it in action by visiting www.BrittAndreatta.com/Wired-to-Resist.

14. The Change Journey Participants

The Change Journey model allows us to distinguish the roles and experiences of all the people involved in a change initiative. We can view the employees as the travelers who must move through the change, while other participants design and lead the process.

Employees: The Travelers

Employees play a vital role in how every change initiative unfolds. They are the travelers on the change journey, no matter its form, and, ultimately, they have to implement and live the changes.

As we discussed in chapter 3, choice and desire have an important impact on employee motivation. We can almost see it as willingness to engage in the effort required and also their ability to generate and maintain forward momentum.

If employees want the change and choose it, you will have a group of people who are excited and willing to go on the change journey. They will be up for the effort required and may even run toward it with enthusiasm. It doesn't mean the change is any less disruptive or will occur more quickly, but their motivation and momentum will be self-driven and positive. Contrast that with a group who doesn't want the change nor did they choose it. They will have low motivation and momentum and will likely be resisting the change and perhaps even digging in their heels.

Managing these two groups will require very different skills and strategies. The Change Journey model allows you to assess employee motivation and convey it through the use of four people icons:

- **Runner:** Desires and chooses change (celebrating the win)
- **Walker:** Desires the change but didn't choose it (embracing the opportunity)
- **Trudger:** Doesn't desire the change but they did choose it (enduring/accepting the situation)
- **Resister:** Neither desires nor chooses the change (digging in heels)

Assessing employee motivation and momentum is crucial because it determines how the leaders should guide the entire rollout, beginning with how they initially communicate the change journey to their

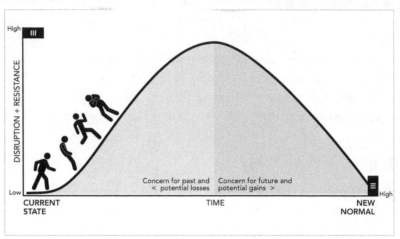

The four types of travelers on the change journey

employees. The assessment should look at the group who will need to go on the journey and estimate which of the four types they will be. Perhaps they are 100 percent of the same type, like the walker who will "embrace the opportunity." Or you might have a mixed group where 50 percent are trudgers who will "endure/accept the situation" and 50 percent are resisters who will dig in their heels.

The Change Journey model helps you see how you need to engage your entire group, allowing you to better anticipate a range of reactions, attitudes, and interteam interactions.

Leader Roles: Expedition Designers, Trailblazers, and Guides

In every change initiative, a relatively small group of people are involved with both the design and implementation. My model articulates each of these key roles so that people can see how they intersect. In looking for an appropriate metaphor, I realized that my own experience on the California AIDS Ride, combined with my friend's summit of Mount Everest, gave me what I needed to clearly illustrate the differences.

The expedition designers identify that change is needed and begin to create the change. For example, the people who first conceived of the California AIDS Ride or of climbing Mount Everest were expedition designers, and often they are involved in the early stages of fleshing out the idea.

At work, expedition designers are often the executives and senior leaders who are guiding the strategy for the future of the organization.

But designers can be mid-level managers and employees, too, since sometimes ideas and plans for change come from the middle or front lines of an organization.

Expedition designers also include the people who develop the change plan. They identify the starting and ending points, plot the route, and work through all the details. In most organizations, the designers are a group of people who collectively figure it all out. They might work together in a coordinated effort through a committee or task force, or they may hand off work to each other as they go. Obviously, designers do most of their work before travelers hear about the change. In fact, by the time a change journey launches, this group is already onto designing the next few change initiatives.

Then there are the trailblazers who set the journey up for success. Trailblazers are crucial to the success of the journey because they are responsible for putting everything in place that will allow the travelers to successfully complete the trek. For example, on Mount Everest, the trailblazers are Sherpas and every expedition has its own dedicated Sherpa group. They start their work before the travelers arrive, summiting the mountain several times as they lay the rope guides and ladders, carrying up vital supplies like oxygen tanks and food, and establishing the base camps and stops where travelers will rest.

The same system applies to, for example, a cycling event, like the California AIDs Ride or the Tour de France. The trailblazers work several months ahead of the actual events, getting everything arranged. Once the ride begins, they are several days ahead of the riders setting up the routes, signs, camps, shower trucks, medical tents, etc. Trailblazers also follow behind the travelers, taking things back down.

In organizations, trailblazers take many forms and often involve key administrative services. For example, IT may need to do a lot of prep work to get things in place so the change initiative goes smoothly. Finance may be working with vendors, approving purchases, and allotting key resources. Learning & Development may be designing training and Facilities may be preparing workspaces.

Finally, you have the guides, the people responsible for getting a specific group of travelers through a change journey. Whether it's a long, intense climb; a quick hike up a steep hill; or a slow, steady trek, the guides play a pivotal role in making sure their group successfully completes the change journey. Guides move with their travelers, tending to a specific group of people. Each guide has a unique experience

The three types of leaders for change journeys

because his or her particular group of travelers has their own unique skills, competencies, and motivations. Good guides watch for and provide what their people need.

I intentionally named this role the guide, rather than the leader, because sometimes guides will be out front but they are more often alongside or even behind their group, providing the right kind of support at the right time.

In most organizations, guides are the leaders or managers responsible for getting their team or direct reports through the change journey. Guides and trailblazers often work in tandem or side-by-side, and people in the administrative services might play both roles. For example, a director in IT or HR might be a trailblazer for the whole organization and then be a guide for their particular team of direct reports. This is difficult to do and requires a lot of effort and focus, which why some teams can experience more change fatigue than others because they are both supporting change and going through it themselves.

The success of all change journeys directly reflects how well people in these roles do their individual jobs and how well they communicate and collaborate with each other. Imagine what would happen if the designers, trailblazers, and guides on the Tour de France were not talking with each other or were not on the same page about the route and its core elements? And what if one of those key people dropped the ball and the water stations were spaced too far apart? Or cars were not blocked from driving on the route? It would be pandemonium and the riders would likely fail. Worse, you could have injuries and even death.

Many of these very issues have occurred during expeditions on Mount Everest over the years. Perhaps the most notable occurred in 1996 when 15 people died in their attempt. The story has been told in documentaries and books, most notably Jon Krakauer's *Into Thin Air* and *The Climb* by Anatoli Boukreev.

While most organizational change journeys are not life threatening, the chaos that comes from poorly designed change or ill-prepared leaders costs billions of dollars, harms employee engagement, and can endanger customer loyalty. And some change initiatives, such as those in healthcare or manufacturing industries, can absolutely threaten life and limb.

Fortunately, with insight and the right preparation, change journeys can be successful. Consider this great example from TMobile. The executives (expedition designers) wanted to become known for their customer service and set about to create an intentional culture shift that would drive the right values and habits among their employees. They planned to measure their success by the number of JD Power Awards they won. Leaders drove a clear and consistent narrative with two transparent goals of increasing customer satisfaction and revenue.

One team of trailblazers across the organization supported the initiative. HR coordinated performance management, expecting every employee to have at least one quarterly goal that was customer focused.

Leaders created accountability by expecting every director to spend two weeks per year in a call center and two more weeks in a retail center. And it was consistently enforced.

To create a culture of recognition, marketing printed blue poker chips that said "#1" on one side and "The Customer Is Why" on the other. Bowls of chips were visible in every office and people gave them to each other to acknowledge effort and improvement.

L&D designed and implemented extensive training for guides and travelers that focused on the core values and behaviors that would support success. Every year, people could nominate employees who exemplified the values for the "PEAK award." The executives selected 150 annual winners who were treated to an all-expenses-paid trip to Hawaii where they celebrated together.

Given this well-thought-out and executed plan, it's not surprising that TMobile not only hit their targets, they exceeded them.

In the next section, we'll focus on additional tips and strategies for both leaders and travelers.

15. Walking Multiple Journeys

As you know, modern change is constant and fast paced, and in reality that means people are often going through several change journeys simultaneously. We can use the Change Journey model to map what that looks like as well: With time running along the horizontal axis, perhaps broken into quarters, you can map your team's changes. This allows you to identify possible problem areas.

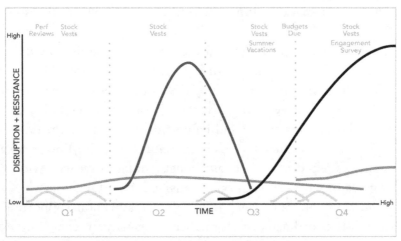

One team's multiple journeys over time

In the example above, the beginning of Q3 is going to be an intense time for this team. They will be cresting a quick hike up a steep hill; halfway through a long, steady trek; sidestepping a pebble on a trail, which might not feel so little at this point; and starting on a long, intense climb. And just a few weeks later, they will add two more pebbles and another long, steady trek just as resistance is building for the long, intense climb. This is important information for the leaders and managers of this team to see. They can now anticipate when the group might be feeling overwhelmed and likely to exhibit signs of stress. They also can see when their leadership and guidance will be most needed. Clearly, they should not be planning their vacations for August!

I recommend that leaders also layer on elements related to the rhythm of their business, such as reviews and peak production periods. This can add additional insights that might cause them to rethink the timing of certain change initiatives or realize they will need to bring on more resources like staffing or administrative support.

For example, if they typically launch their major new product campaign in January, the leaders can anticipate that the heavy lifting of that work will occur when the team is holding a long, intense climb and two long, steady treks. If the team is experiencing change fatigue as well as high disruption and resistance, how creative can you expect them to be? It might or might not be an issue, but now it can be flagged and addressed.

The model can also be used to give you a view across the organization. By seeing the various types of changes rolling out for each function, you can identify potential challenges and where interdepartmental relationships or collaboration might be impacted.

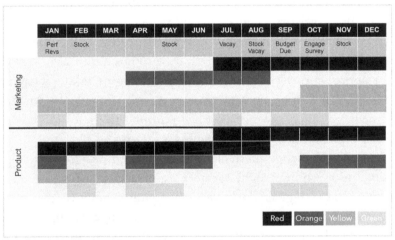

Mapping change across the organization

It can also give you a sense of bandwidth. In this example above, the bandwidth of the product team is going to be pushed several times during the year. It is likely that January and February as well as April through August will be more intense for the team. Whereas the marketing team will be pushed July through November if these current changes stay where they are anticipated.

When teams are maxing on their bandwidth, you are likely to see more reactive emotions, which can create miscommunication and conflict. If these two teams have to work together in July or August, the leaders of both groups will need to provide a lot of support and guidance or better yet, shift some of these pressures beforehand to create better balance.

Change Traffic Control

This mapping exercise usually brings to light something really important. Most of the time, leaders are surprised to see how much change is happening at one time. This is especially true for larger organizations where there are multiple departments driving change.

It's very typical that Facilities is rolling out space planning changes that affect where people work. This could include moving to a new location, remodeling to an open-concept work area, or even changing lighting and desk height.

Separately, HR is driving changes for talent development, perhaps revising the performance review process or redesigning the org structure in ways that change who people report to. IT could be upgrading to a new data platform that everyone uses to track hours and vacation or switching to a different system of productivity tools for file sharing. Finance could be moving to a new purchase order system or vendor approval process. They could be adding or taking away perks and benefits or instituting new processes and procedures. Marketing might be targeting a new customer, with implications for global operation, languages, and currencies. The list goes on and on.

The point is, while these changes have been designed to help the business, poor timing might create a ripple effect of problems that undermine the very goals the business is trying to achieve, or the problem that it's trying to solve. We have all lived through examples of good changes gone bad. A key training is scheduled when the sales team is in their end-of-year push or IT changes the software a week before a major product rollout to customers.

This is why I recommend that your organization appoint a person to serve as the air traffic controller of change, much like the role at airports who keep planes from crashing into each other. If someone is responsible for tracking changes and considering possible challenges and unintended consequences, the more likely you are to stop an unnecessary disaster. This person should also leverage all available data analytics. For example, you already have a process for entering a new reporting relationship. What if that process could flag when a person or team has had two manager changes in a short period of time? You already have a method for tracking where people work and could flag excessive workplace shifts. You get the idea.

Once someone is tracking and mapping, it becomes easy to identify small shifts that can make all the difference. Sometimes, combining two changes together can be a great solution. Sometimes delaying or moving a change by a few weeks can have a profound effect on its success.

It's not unlike how we can track weather and create an early warning system. The change traffic controller can quickly become a vital role in every organization because she or he can help identify potential challenges—and help ensure sure that employees and leaders are prepared for what is coming.

Your Learning Journey

Take a few moments to apply these concepts to changes coming your way in the next 12 months.

- Map them out on a timeline. Which type of change journey best represents each of the changes you will be going through? Is it a pebble on the trail; a long, steady trek; a quick hike up a steep hill; or long and intense climb?
- Next, consider your motivation for each of the change journeys and give each one the stick figure that best represents your desire and choice. Are you running or walking toward it, trudging through it, or resisting it?
- Finally, identify who the players are for each journey. Who designed each expedition? Which people are serving as trailblazers? Who will be your guide? And who are your fellow travelers?

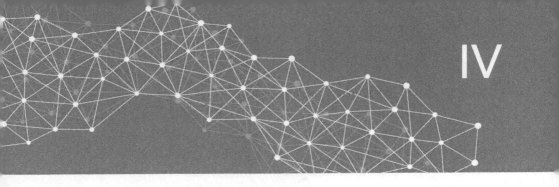

IV

THRIVING THROUGH CHANGE:
STRATEGIES FOR SUCCESS

16. Tips for Travelers

Throughout your working life, you will be in the role of traveler many times. We all find ourselves on the receiving end of change journeys, many of which we did not choose and may not want. Even top executives must respond to requests by their shareholders and demands of the market, not to mention regulatory bodies and climate change.

But every traveler has the opportunity to thrive through change, even difficult changes that are foisted on you despite your protests. Let's look at how you can empower yourself to move through all kinds of changes with grace and style.

Do an Inventory

First thing, take stock of your situation. By taking a few moments to assess things, you will be better prepared to respond to many different changes.

1. Consider what kind of change is coming your way. How much disruption it is likely to cause? Does it impact how and where you will do your work? Does it impact your team of colleagues and relationship network? Will it require new skills and habits? Do you have to give up well-grooved habits? This information will help you plot along the vertical axis of the change journey and estimate how high a peak you can expect to climb. Look at how long it will take to acclimate to the change (not just getting over the major hump of the change but to complete it, getting to the new normal). It is weeks? Months? Or even years?

2. Add at least 50 percent to your estimate. I'm not kidding. Give yourself a good healthy cushion because even your leaders cannot accurately predict what the change is going to look like and if you estimate high, you won't be thrown when their estimates are off. It's not uncommon for workplace initiatives to take twice or even three times the estimated resources and time. If you given yourself a cushion, you won't be thrown by it. This works for kitchen remodels too. I'm just sayin'. . . .

3. From your newly adjusted assessment of disruption and acclimation, determine which of the four change journeys you are embarking on. The long, intense climb (red), the quick hike up a steep hill (orange), a long, steady trek (yellow), or a pebble on the trail (green). Since it's likely that the small, slight obstacle of a pebble is not keeping you up at night, I'm only going to focus on the other three as we continue.

4. Map the next 12 months for all the change journeys you will be traveling. This includes those at work and those at home because we do not have two brains or two bodies. Your change bandwidth will be tapped into by all changes, professional and personal, so map them on the same timeline to get the bigger view. Don't forget to note some "rhythm of business" elements like annual reviews and budget submissions and some "rhythm of life" elements like birthday parties, vacations, and taxes.

5. For each change journey, choose the stick figure that represents your change motivation: If it's something you choose and desire, use the running figure. If it's something you want but did not choose, use the walker. Or you can use the trudger or resister. This is also a great time to consider if you can shift your attitude about a change. Can you find something to look forward to, a possible gain that might motivate you? Will it be an opportunity to

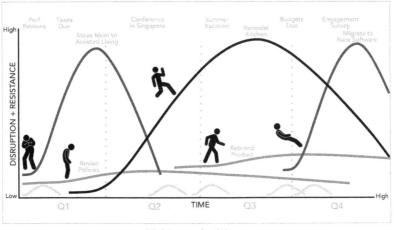

Taking stock of change

develop a new skill or make new friends? You can actually do a lot to shift your orientation by choosing to look for something good or positive. Try it and see if you can shift some of your stick figures from one type to another.

6. In the yearlong view, when will you be carrying the most changes (full bandwidth)? This is likely when you will experience change fatigue. Also, note when things will be lighter, as these are moments of possible rest and recovery. Most importantly, can you make any adjustments? I can't tell you how helpful this view has been for me and the groups I work with. Just by seeing the big picture, you can identify where things are stacking up and sometimes, you can shift something by just a few weeks, which makes all the difference.

7. After you have adjusted what you can, the final step is to circle or highlight the times when things are going to be the most intense. These are the times when you need to be intentional about how you support yourself so you can thrive.

A Powerful Troika of Support: Self-Care, Mindfulness, and Play

Once you have taken stock of your change journeys, you can intentionally mitigate the effects. Remember, the brain science of change tells us that our amygdala will perceive change as dangerous, kicking up fear and anxiety. Here comes Chicken Little! We might also feel lost, especially if the change will impact our physical space or social networks, causing our entorhinal cortex to do extra work to build new maps. If we have to learn new skills or habits, our basal ganglia will need some time to get enough repetitions to build a new automated habit. And finally, if we experience failure, our habenula is going to suppress good feelings and possibly even physical movement.

Keep in mind, change in general brings up some predictable worries for people. Dr. David Rock, of the NeuroLeadership Institute, created the SCARF Model that shows the five areas that people focus on, particularly when under stress:

- **S**tatus: Our sense of importance in relation to others
- **C**ertainty: Our ability to predict the future
- **A**utonomy: Our sense of control over events

- **R**elatedness: A measure of our trust of others
- **F**airness: Our perception of how fair or equal things are

According to Rock's research, humans naturally sort for these, and they are wired to move toward experiences that improve these aspects and away from those that threaten them.

I had a firsthand experience of the SCARF model during the acquisition. As I was feeling emotions like fear, excitement, anxiety, confusion, and hope, I realized that the source was status, certainty, etc. One minute, I'd be excited about my new role and the next I was worrying I would report to someone my junior. One moment, I would be curious about the team I was joining and the next I was stressed they wouldn't get who I am and what I bring to the table.

Even though I understood what I was going through (I teach this stuff!), I couldn't help myself from thinking these thoughts and having these worries. The power of our biology is stronger than education, experience, and expertise combined.

The only thing that got me through the crazy year was using what I call the powerful troika of support. Because I was going through an intense bevy of change journeys, I knew it was on me to take care of myself if I was to be my best through it all. That's not to say I was awesome, however. I had anxious and cranky days—but whatever state I was in, I know it was ten times better than I would have been without the troika of self-care, mindfulness, and play.

Self-Care
This includes the basics: good nutrition, sufficient sleep and exercise. We all know these are good things to do for our bodies but during times of stress, they become even more important.

As I mentioned in chapter 11 on the habenula, a body responds to stress as if it's being attacked and our immune system tries to fight the invisible foe like it would the flu. In fact, I liken starting on a change journey to the beginning of flu season. When flu season starts, most of us make choices to strengthen our immune systems. We eat more veggies and cut back on sugar. We exercise, which actually increases serotonin, the feel-good chemical. And we get more sleep.

Sleep should not be underrated as a tool in your self-care arsenal. Harvard Medical School has an entire division dedicated to "sleep medicine" and the profound effect sleep has on mood, focus, and mental performance among other things. The Centers for Disease Control and Prevention report that not getting enough sleep is linked to a range of chronic conditions including diabetes, obesity, and depression.

Further, a study published in *Science* magazine estimated that even one extra hour of sleep can boost happiness, especially for people who are not getting enough. Better sleep has been associated with weight loss, enhanced creativity, and better performance at work.

In her book *Brain Science for Principals*, Dr. Linda Lyman outlines the crucial role that sleep plays in how we move new learning into memory, a topic I also cover in my book *Wired to Grow*. In fact, the National Institutes of Health state "Sleep deficiency can cause problems with learning, focusing, and reacting. You may have trouble making decisions, solving problems, remembering things, controlling your emotions and behavior, and coping with change." Most change requires new learning so sleep not only helps us address the stress of change but helps us build new habits more quickly.

Mindfulness

Another way we prepare for flu season is getting a flu shot, which inoculates us against the harmful effects of the virus. Mindfulness inoculates us against the harmful effects of change and can be an antidote for the stress that often accompanies change. Whether it's meditation, yoga, being present, or expressing gratitude, mindfulness plays a powerful role in our brains. There is a reason that every wisdom tradition since the beginning of history purports some type of mindfulness practice.

Dr. Richard Davidson, Professor and Director of the Waisman Laboratory for Brain Imaging and Behavior at the University of Wisconsin, studies the effects of mindfulness on the brain. He uses MRI

Powerful tools for thriving through change

technology to compare the brains of long-time meditators, like Tibetan monks, to people who have never meditated, and those who have just done their first-ever meditation. The results are astounding. Meditating even *one time* permanently changes the brain in a measurable way. He details more benefits in his book *The Emotional Life of Your Brain*.

His groundbreaking research has shown that people who meditate are able to focus longer, they are less likely to worry about future events, and when something stressful does happen, they experience less distress in the moment and return quickly to their normal state. Another study by Dr. Sara Lazar at the Harvard University Medical School found that a daily mindfulness practice actually shrinks the amygdala, making it less reactive in as little as eight weeks.

In addition, several studies have shown that both gratitude and mindfulness make the brain more receptive to learning, which is vital during change, as we gain new skills and habits. Dr. Alex Korb synthesized some of the key findings on gratitude in his *Psychology Today* article titled "The Grateful Brain: The Neuroscience of Giving Thanks." Studies have shown that intentional gratitude practices boost attention, determination, and enthusiasm and reduce anxiety, depression, and physical ailments.

Because of these and many other compelling studies, I also began a daily meditation practice of 15 minutes per day. I have seen a huge shift in my own reactivity and ability to manage all kinds of stress, including change. If you have not yet explored mindfulness, I encourage you to check out Desk-Yogi.com. It turns your computer or smartphone into a mindfulness station. A lot of companies are buying Desk-Yogi for their employees so it's also something you can suggest to your HR department.

Time magazine recently published a special edition completely dedicated to mindfulness ("Mindfulness: The New Science of Health and Happiness"), which compiled the latest studies on mindfulness practices with tips about how to incorporate them into your everyday routine. It gives the details on how mindfulness improves health, including lowering or reducing anxiety, blood pressure, and weight, and increasing or improving happiness and sleep. It also showcases companies who have integrated mindfulness into the workplace like Google, LinkedIn, and the Huffington Post.

Play

Studies have shown that people who play are more adaptive, innovative, and have more positive relationships. And the benefits don't just stop there. According to the National Institute for Play, play is vital for human health and well-being. It generates optimism, spurs curiosity, fosters empathy, cultivates perseverance, and leads to mastery. Conversely, societies, families, and other cultures that maintain a prolonged deprivation of play experience increased depression, stress-related diseases, addictions, and interpersonal violence.

Creativity and play also go hand in hand. When we play, we let ourselves move into a physical and emotional state that allows our creativity to flow more naturally. Our logical and analytical left brain takes a break so our right brain can start making all kinds of insightful connections.

Neuroscience has demonstrated that playful environments powerfully shape the cerebral cortex, the part of the brain where the highest level of cognitive processing takes place. So, it makes sense that not playing much stifles creative energy. Dr. Stuart Brown, author of *Play: How It Shapes the Brain, Opens the Imagination, and Invigorates the Soul* has identified seven patterns of play. Consider your experiences with each, from childhood to adulthood:

- **Attunement play:** This occurs between infants and their parents/caregivers. As they look at each other, they naturally smile and connect, becoming attuned to each other.
- **Body play:** This occurs through movement and is how we learn to coordinate our bodies. Children naturally enjoy this process and, as we grow, we expand to more complex movement like sports and dance with increasing precision and control.
- **Object play:** This is how we play with things. It begins with simple things like banging on a pan or bouncing a ball and increases in complexity as we develop dexterity. Videogames, painting, and cooking are forms of object play.
- **Social play:** What we do with others for fun. From simple hide-and-seek and wrestling to complex group games, social play creates the base for interpersonal relationships, collaboration, and empathy.
- **Imaginative play:** This is the source of much creativity. It starts with simple pretend play in childhood, as we take on

characters (for example, firefighter or teacher) and extends to fantastical creations of made-up worlds, friends, languages, and situations.

- **Narrative play:** This involves storytelling and is how we make sense of the world and our place in it. Storytelling is part of every culture and allows us to cross concepts of time and space as well as access various emotional states.

- **Creative play:** This occurs when we use our sense of fantasy or imagination to transcend or transform what is currently known to a new state. Musicians and dancers often use creative play to develop new works. Einstein was known for using this kind of play to consider unproven scientific ideas.

Play has healing properties as well. Charlie Hoehn, author of *Play It Away: A Workaholic's Cure for Anxiety*, used to suffer from intense and debilitating panic attacks. He found that play was a big part of his healing process.

So find a way to build more play into your life. It can be simple and solitary or complex and collaborative. The most important thing: make it fun. You should have a good play session at least once per week—and more is better. If you need more motivation, consider this quote by Dr. Stuart Brown: "The opposite of play is not work. It's depression."

Be an Active Participant

In addition to the powerful troika, one of the most important ways to ensure you thrive during change is to become an active participant in the journey. If you stay passive and let the change "be done" to you, you allow the brain's natural resistance to take over. And that doesn't benefit you in the long run because it increases anxiety and fatigue, and decreases the feel-good chemicals. This harms your health and well-being both at work and when you're off the clock.

If you can find a way to turn toward the change with a "Let's do this!" attitude, you can now engage in problem-solving, turn on your creativity, and feel more empowered. You also can do a better job of getting what you need to thrive. While I would love to promise you that your leaders and managers are going to do a great job, we know that you might end up with an inexperienced expedition designer or an inept guide. (If you do, please buy them a copy of this book.) But don't let their competence get in the way of your experience.

Here are my ten tips for being an active participant in your journey:

1. **Learn about the journey:** Once change is announced, find out all that you can so that your brain can begin processing the news. The sooner you orient yourself to the journey and your role as a traveler, the easier it will become.

2. **Ask questions:** If you need more information, ask for it. If something is not clear, ask for clarity. In the next chapters I share things leaders can do to create successful change. I encourage all travelers to read those sections too because it will supply you with good questions to ask or suggestions to make, especially if your guide is not proactively addressing them.

3. **Find your own purpose:** Your ability to be motivated and happy will increase if you can create your own meaningful purpose for the journey. Find a way to convert the change to something that matters to you.

4. **Partner up:** You are not the only one going through this change so find a trek buddy or create a team. You will all benefit from sharing information, leaning on each other, and cheering each other's successes.

5. **Build a roadmap:** Most change plans are long, detailed documents that aren't really helpful. Create your own visual map of the journey. Draw the milestones, the steep sections, and the resting places. This can be fun (and enlightening) to do with your travel team as well.

6. **Gamify the experience:** The reward part of our brain loves games and prizes. Gold stars and high fives matter. Find a way to turn the journey into a series of levels that you earn points or stars for completing, and give yourself cool rewards for hitting milestones. This can be a great thing to do with coworkers. You can even turn a negative experience into something fun. For example, before the holidays my friends and I play "dysfunctional family bingo." We make a bingo card with all the things we hope won't happen like "Uncle George comments on my weight," or "Mom insults Grandma." Then as the weekend unfolds, we mark the

Ten ways for travelers to be active participants

squares and text each other. Later, we all go out for dinner and treat the winner. This tradition has made the holidays much more fun and the camaraderie makes it easier for us to love our families as they are. And you can see the brain science working through problem-solving, finding success and rewards. If you are struggling with change at work, turn it in to a positive game. Perhaps you get a star for helping someone out, or you create a "no complaining" rule, with the first person to complain buying the others lunch. Maybe you create teams and have a friendly competition for the fastest or most creative solution. Find ways to gamify it and you will feel much better.

7. **Train for the trek:** Like any journey, training can help you build your strength and stamina before the trail gets difficult. And having the right shoes can help too. If you approached your change journey with the same idea, how might you get ready to be successful? Perhaps you attend the training early and get some additional coaching. If your organization doesn't offer it, look to other sources like books and online training sites like LinkedIn Learning or Udemy. Perhaps you invest in some new equipment like a good planner or a subscription to Desk-Yogi.com. Maybe there are wise mentors you can speak with. Like most things, training can be more fun when done with a group, so consider how you can invite others to join you.

8. **Rest at the resting points:** Travelers often make the mistake of trudging on when they could rest, thinking something like, *I'll get done quicker if I just keep going. Resting is a waste of time.* But rest is really important for combatting our brain's natural resistance. Every change journey has slower times or flat sections before the next steep hill. Take advantage of them. We live in such a busy culture now that we often don't know what to do with periods of quiet, so we fill them. We take on a project at home, or we push harder on something at work. But rest is vital, so give yourself permission to take a break. These are great times to double down on the powerful troika of self-care, mindfulness, and play.

9. **Ask for help when you need it:** Another mistake travelers make is not taking advantage of available assistance. They keep pushing through hoping things will just get better. But often they don't. If you are feeling overwhelmed or fatigued or confused, ask for help! Often organizations put various support systems in place. Make sure you note what they are and how to access them.

10. **If you need to, get off the mountain:** Occasionally, a change journey might just be too much. This usually happens when a person is carrying several intense change journeys at the same time, and likely a combination of things from work and at home. Life happens—you or a loved one might become ill or injured, or perhaps you just had a baby, or an elderly parent needs assistance, or you've been a victim of a crime. If you're unable to participate in the change, talk to your manager and HR to discuss your options. Perhaps you can sit this one out or play a less intense role. If not, maybe you can take time away. This is why organizations often allow leaves of absence, to take care of employees during times when things are just too much. Sometimes bowing out is the best thing you can do for yourself, your team, and your organization.

Overall, I hope that you can see travelers are not just passive passengers in the change journey. Even when many of the details are out of your control, there are lots of things you can do to ensure that you not only survive but thrive.

17. The Leader's Toolkit

Based on my research on the neuroscience of change, I have created a leader's toolkit that will help you move your travelers through any kind of change journey. It works with the brain, particularly addressing the four structures of the amygdala, entorhinal cortex, basal ganglia, and habenula. This toolkit also takes into account the various factors that influence a traveler's motivation and momentum.

The toolkit has three main types of tools: navigation tools, motivation tools, and connection tools, which can be applied together in different combinations to meet your travelers' needs on their respective journeys. Let's open up this backpack of goodies and see what's in it.

Navigation Tools: The Why and How of the Journey

The change journey is no different from any other traveling experience—it's an exercise in navigating through time and space. Travelers of all kinds are much more likely to get to their destinations safely if they have the right navigation tools. Hikers use geographic contour maps, compasses, and trail guides, while airline pilots use aviation charts and GPS systems. All of these tools should be incorporated into your change rollout and communication plan.

Start with Why
Before you start on any journey, you should know why you are going in the first place. If you don't know the why up front, you are missing a key element to good decision-making and motivation. And the purpose should not only be clear to you. You need to communicate the why to your travelers. Simon Sinek's book, *Start with Why*, says it all: Travelers need to know why they need to make the journey at all. In fact, the why is the center of what Sinek calls "the golden circle" that includes the how and the what. But the why must come first.

From the brain science perspective, knowing the why helps the amygdala perceive change as less threatening and helps travelers look into the future and anticipate potential gains. In fact, the more you spell out the purpose and potential gains for them, the sooner they can shift their focus.

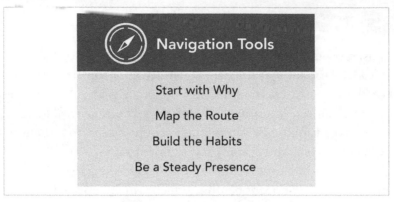

Navigation Tools

Start with Why

Map the Route

Build the Habits

Be a Steady Presence

The leader's toolkit for navigating

Map the Route

Once you know the why, you need to map your route. Getting from point A to point B requires you to identify each point's location and the best route between them. Most of today's change journeys are from a current state to a new, presumably better, future state. So the map might be expressed in gained revenue, decreased complaints, or any other metrics that matter to your business. However you explain it, as the leader you have to tell people where they're headed and place a beacon there to guide them.

Creating a map of the journey is critical to your travelers' success because it keeps them from getting lost and it can also help them track their progress, boosting their sense of accomplishment. Like all good maps, it helps if you can add milestones and sign posts along the way, again to help keep people on track and give them a sense of progress and accomplishment. And taking the entorhinal cortex into account, if the journey will affect your traveler's physical workspace or social network you will want to create literal maps of places and people too.

Build the Habits

It's highly likely that your change journey will require travelers to change their habits and behaviors in some way. This should be called out in your change rollout and communication plan. What, specifically, do your travelers need to be doing and saying? Get really crisp on the words and actions. The returns on developing this level of specificity can't be overstated, because it gives your travelers the right learning and training. Think about the new habits you need them to build. What is the cue, the routine, and the reward? This is all the work of the basal ganglia and we can either make it easier or harder for it to do its job of building habits.

Remember, repetition matters. A neural pathway is built and strengthened through repetitions and a habit is formed around 40 to 50. Use the power of training and practice to get those habits built quickly. Practice is how we hone and improve our skills, developing mastery. because we all gain so much from the *doing* of something.

One of my favorite tools is Practice.xyz, which uses the power of interactive video to demonstrate ideal behaviors as well as create an environment for learners to receive authentic assessment and coaching.

You can also use technology to create realistic practice environments for people. Explore the benefits of immersive training with companies like Mursion and Cubic. Check out the agility of adaptive learning with Amplifier and Area 9. And consider the power of virtual reality with providers like SilVR Thread and Virtalis.

Be a Steady Presence
Navigation tools should be reliable and consistent. Because change can be so disruptive, you want your navigation tools to become the new source of constancy for your travelers. Every great leader will tell you that this is what makes the difference—being a reliable and steady presence, repeating the key information over and over. You will need to repeat things more often than you expect and you might feel like you are a broken record sometimes. You will also find that you need to keep it up longer than you expect. So many leaders have told me that the biggest mistake they made was letting up after the group got over the hump of resignation. The travelers showed signs of embracing the change so they relaxed. And the group backslid. Think of your role like you are building a guide rope that they can hold on to whenever they need.

Motivation: Recognition and Rewards

The leader's toolkit also offers tools to motivate your travelers. Motivation is very important for combatting the brain's natural resistance to change. It helps to address the various emotions that are part of the transition. Unless you are blessed with a group that has high choice and desire for the change, you will need to use various forms of recognition and rewards.

Focus on the Purpose

Humans are wired to seek purpose. This is part of the "become" aspect of our biology. In Dan Pink's book *Drive*, he synthesized many studies on human motivation and shows that people are motivated by three things: purpose, along with autonomy and mastery (more on those below). People naturally want to make a contribution, so if you spell out the bigger purpose that the change initiative achieves, you'll naturally tap into your travelers' motivation.

In fact, purpose is so important that companies are shifting to be more purpose-driven. Books like *The Purpose Economy*, *Start Something That Matters*, *Firms of Endearment*, and *We First* all share compelling evidence that both consumers and employees are seeking businesses that have a positive and meaningful impact in the world.

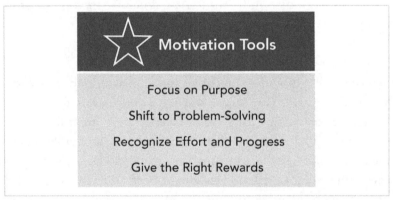

Motivation Tools

Focus on Purpose

Shift to Problem-Solving

Recognize Effort and Progress

Give the Right Rewards

The leader's toolkit for motivating

In *Purpose at Work: The Largest Global Study on the Role of Purpose in the Workforce* (2016 Workforce Purpose Index), researchers state that connecting employees with purpose increased employee engagement, productivity, and profit. They found that purpose-driven employees feel 64 percent higher levels of fulfillment in their work, are 50 percent more likely to be in leadership positions, and are 47 percent more likely to promote their company as a good place to work.

The other two sources that Dan Pink identified were autonomy, the ability to be self-directed, and mastery, the opportunity to get better at things. Both of these can be threatened or decreased during a change journey, which makes purpose even more important. So, consider how you can connect the change initiative to a larger purpose, either some greater good the organization is trying to achieve, or to a personal value that the employee holds.

Shift from Goals to Problem-Solving

One way to motivate employees is to shift your focus from goals to problem-solving. According to Dr. Kyra Bobinet, a professor at Stanford University, "Goals are typically outcome-oriented, which means we either succeed in our attempts to achieve them—or we fail. If we 'fail' at something, the habenula kills our incentive to give things another go." Problem-solving works with the reward-seeking part of the brain. As we seek and find a solution, the experience becomes a success, something that works with both the habenula and basal ganglia. In addition, problem-solving is a type of design thinking, where we tinker and adjust as we experiment, getting better with each iteration.

Consider how most change plans are constructed. Most have rigid goals and milestones and rarely, if ever, do they unfold as expected, turning the change journey into a series of failures. To avoid this, frame each phase of the change initiative as an exercise in problem-solving. This allows your travelers to become active participants in the journey rather than passengers. And it's likely that their experience and perspective will improve the change initiative in countless ways.

Problem-solving also helps to shift employees from a fixed mindset to a growth mindset. Stanford psychologist Dr. Carol Dweck's research has examined what differentiates people who succeed from those who don't. She found that people who don't succeed tend to have a fixed mindset, meaning that they believe that their inherent traits or characteristics—such as their IQ (intelligence quotient) or people skills—are set once they reach adulthood.

Fixed Mindset leads to a desire to look good so tends to:	Growth Mindset leads to a desire to learn so tends to:
Believe that most skills are based on traits that are fixed and cannot change	Believe that skills can always improve with hard work
See effort as unnecessary; something to do when you're not good enough	See effort as a path to mastery and therefore essential
Avoid challenges because could reveal lack of skill; tends to give up easily	Embrace challenges and see them as opportunity to grow
See feedback as personally threatening to sense of self and gets defensive	See feedback as useful for learning and improving
View setbacks as discouraging; tends to blame others	View setbacks as a wake-up call to work harder next time
Feel threatened by the success of others; may undermine others in effort to look good	Find lessons and inspiration in the success of others
As a result, they may plateau early and achieve less than their full potential.	*As a result, they reach ever-higher levels of potential and performance.*

The two mindsets at work

A person with a fixed mindset thinks, *I've got what I've got and I just have to make the most of it, but I can't change it.* In contrast, a person with a growth mindset believes that they can always get better, that they can always learn something new, or practice something more, and that studying and effort are the pathways to improvement and even mastery. A person with a growth mindset thinks, *I may not be able to do this yet, but I can work hard and get better.*

The growth mindset yields all kinds of other benefits too. Look at the above chart comparing the two mindsets at work. You can see that mindset influences how we view everything from effort, challenges, and feedback to the success of others.

Because of the compelling research on growth mindset, a lot of organizations are rethinking their performance review processes, moving away from ratings, and instead focusing on growth and improvement. When we rate people as "average," "excellent," or "poor," we essentially replicate the fixed mindset and say, "You are what you are." But when we move to evaluating growth and improvement, we activate motivation and, ultimately, potential, saying, "You are what you reach for."

In fact, the hallmark word of the growth mindset is *yet*. As in, "I haven't mastered that yet, but I will." It instantly turns a negative phrase into one of possibility and potential. As the leader of a change journey, harness the power of yet in your own messaging.

Recognize Effort and Progress

A key way to motivate your travelers is to recognize both effort and progress. Recognizing effort is part of fostering a growth mindset, which creates a culture of learning. Here are some examples for how feedback looks when it activates fixed and growth mindsets. Notice

Fixed (ability)	Growth (effort + improvement)
"Great job! You are so smart."	"Great job! I can tell you put a lot of time into that."
"You are really talented at this."	"You really applied yourself."
"You did high-quality work."	"I like the way you review and improve your work. That extra step makes all the difference."
"See, I told you it would be easy. You're a natural at this."	"You worked hard and did a great job. I think you're ready for something more challenging."
"You rocked it!"	"It was a long, complex project, but you stuck to it and got it done. You rocked it!"
"Nice job finishing the project."	"I'm really proud of you and how you kept trying even when it got hard. That persistence really paid off."

Feedback in both fixed and growth mindset forms

that fixed mindset tends to frame feedback in terms of a trait whereas growth feedback focuses on effort and improvement.

During a change journey, you will have lots of opportunities to recognize effort and improvement and doing so will give your team a boost. This can be especially helpful for the travelers who did not want or choose the change and might be trudging along or digging in their heels. The more their effort is rewarded, the more likely both the basal ganglia and habenula will respond in ways that assist the change journey.

But don't ignore your walkers and runners if you are blessed to have them. They will also benefit from recognition, giving them a boost that may energize the entire group. In fact, in the *2015 Employee Recognition Report* conducted by Globoforce, researchers found that employee recognition boosted engagement, retention, wellness, safety, and employer brand.

You can recognize your travelers in many different ways as recognition is generally a type of reward that the brain responds well to. Certainly, a word from you, their leader, is powerful, so don't underestimate the power of your praise. According to Dr. Donald Clifton, co-author of *How Full Is Your Bucket*, not feeling appreciated is the number one reason employees leave a job. In addition, a study by Deloitte found that organizations with effective employee recognition programs had 31 percent less turnover than those with ineffective ones. In 2016, OfficeVibe conducted a global study of over one thousand organizations in more than 150 countries. In their report, *The Global & Real-Time State of Employee Engagement*, they share the following results:

- 65 percent of employees feel like they don't get enough praise
- 82 percent of employees think it's better to give someone praise than a gift
- 35 percent of employees have to wait more than three months to get feedback from their manager
- 82 percent of employees really appreciate receiving feedback, regardless if it's positive or negative
- 62 percent of employees say they wish they received more feedback from their colleagues

Since being recognized by peers also matters, you can create opportunities for that to happen, perhaps in meetings about the change journey. See if you can create a culture where everyone is on the lookout for effort and improvement and make it a positive and playful part of the journey. Look for websites and apps to try out, or even go old school with high fives and gold stars if that works for your culture and context.

Marking progress is another part of this process. Like any journey, your team needs to know where they are on the map, what they have already completed, and what's coming next. Think again of climbing expeditions to Everest or the Tour de France. Every single inch of the process is mapped out and teams spend every evening discussing what happened during the day and plotting their strategy for the next. Climbers and cyclists need to know this information so they can manage their energy and make the right choices with food and hydration, or even when and how to nurse an injury.

Your travelers are no different. By communicating regularly about the roadmap and their progress, you empower employees to become active participants in the journey, especially if you view each leg of the trek as a phase of problem-solving. Also, progress needs to be celebrated! As your team crosses the milestones of the change journey, be sure you acknowledge each and every one with some sort of recognition. Even if you are behind schedule or over budget, you must find ways to mark progress and celebrate. Otherwise, the habenula is likely to code the experience a "failure" and your travelers will become resistant to future change initiatives.

This doesn't mean that you don't have honest conversations about performance and quality. You must have those too. But also be sure you build in moments that let people know they're making progress even though you're not there yet. Too many leaders give too much weight to the constructive and critical feedback and bypass the celebrations because they are busy or behind, leaving the brain with nothing to interpret as reward.

A process from *The Four Disciplines of Execution* by Chris McChesney, Sean Covey and Jim Huling is one of my favorite ways to ensure that progress is properly measured and recognized. It is very effective for driving all kinds of results, whether it's a change initiative or not. These are the four disciplines:

1. Focus on the wildly important goals.
2. Act on the lead measures.
3. Keep a compelling scoreboard.
4. Create a cadence of accountability.

This effective process helps leaders get clear on their metrics of success and "gamifies" them so that employees are both motivated to hit those metrics and take ownership of them. The process includes learning from failures (growth mindset) as well as celebrating successes.

Use the Right Rewards

Recognition and praise are definitely rewards but they are not the only ones. Remember, rewards play two vital roles in the neuroscience of change: (1) they help the habenula code an experience as a success, rather than a failure that it will try to avoid, and (2) they help the brain to want to replicate the behavior, because the basal ganglia sees rewards as the third component in the habit loop.

Charles Duhigg, in his book *The Power of Habit*, compiled and synthesized studies on habit formation from MIT, Columbia University, and other institutions. All kinds of rewards can work. Social connection is a powerful reward because we respond to acknowledgment and encouragement. Getting that "Good job!" makes the basal ganglia very happy. When human skin touches human skin—think high five, pat on the back, or hug—our brain releases oxytocin, a feel-good chemical the basal ganglia loves.

And, of course, prizes, points, and chocolate work too. Rewards do not need to be big or showy, they just need to mark a success and be meaningful for your travelers. If you don't know what those are, ask them. By discussing rewards with them, you engage them in problem-solving and increase your change journey's likelihood of success.

Over the years, I have seen teams create all kinds of rewards. For example, ringing a loud gong when a goal has been hit or earning gold stars or blue chips, which become a symbol of pride. Gift cards are great too and can range from $5 to $5000. The most successful models seem to have two levels. The first includes small tokens that mark recognition or success, like stars or chips, verbal "shoutouts" or electronic kudos. These should be given out abundantly but authentically. The second level includes larger, special prizes that are given to a few who show exemplary performance, like TMobile's PEAK achievement award. The latter requires a nomination and selection process because it's vital that the system feels fair and accurately acknowledge top performing teams and individuals.

Again, all of this will be most effective if it reflects what is most meaningful to your travelers.

Connection Tools: Patience and Empathy

Connection tools are powerful because they help build rapport and collaboration between and among your travelers. As we know, change can be a disruptive and difficult process that can trigger worry, anxiety, and fear. And moving through change requires risk-taking and vulnerability. So, building a team culture of trust and empathy is key to bringing out the best in your travelers.

Start with Empathy

Because the transition aspect of change is such an emotional process, the biggest tool in your kit is empathy. Dr. Daniel Goleman, author of *Emotional Intelligence* and codirector of the Consortium for Research on Emotional Intelligence in Organizations at Rutgers University, identifies empathy as one of the core skills for building relationships with others. Emotional intelligence, or EQ, is what differentiates highly successful people from others.

According to Theresa Wiseman, a professor at the University of Southampton, empathy has four qualities:

1. Being able to see the world as others see it
2. Being nonjudgmental
3. Recognizing another's feelings
4. Communicating your understanding of that person's feelings

Dr. Brené Brown, scholar and author of *Daring Greatly*, says empathy is "feeling with people." In fact, she claims that empathy is often an act of vulnerability because in order to make an authentic connection with another person, we have to identify that same feeling in ourselves. That might be easy for feelings like hope and joy but much more difficult for feelings like anxiety, frustration, and fear.

Empathy can be learned, and as a leader you must learn it if you want to support your travelers and ensure their (and your) success. You can also help your travelers develop empathy so that they support each other. I weave empathy and emotional intelligence into all of my leadership development and manager-training programs, including those on change.

Empathy does more than drive positive relationships. It is one of the two key components that create psychological safety.

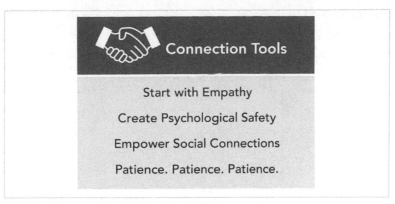

Connection Tools

Start with Empathy

Create Psychological Safety

Empower Social Connections

Patience. Patience. Patience.

The leader's toolkit for connecting

Create Psychological Safety

The tech company Google studied hundreds of its teams around the world and found that psychological safety was what differentiated the best teams from the rest. Harvard researcher Dr. Amy Edmondson defines psychological safety as "a sense of confidence that the team will not embarrass, reject or punish someone for speaking up—it is a shared belief held by members of a team that the team is safe for interpersonal risk-taking. It describes a team climate characterized by interpersonal trust and mutual respect in which people are comfortable being themselves."

Google's study further identified that the who of a team is not relevant—it's the how: not who they are but how they work together. A productive team builds psychological safety through empathy and making sure that all members contribute equally, allowing every person's ideas and thoughts to be heard, and contributing to the collective success of the whole.

If you are leading a change journey, help create psychological safety by making sure you build a culture of empathy. Model empathy when you engage with your travelers and help them do the same. In addition, make sure that meetings allow for each person to be heard and enable equal sharing. It's not enough to just ask if anyone has something to say. You have to make it safe and easy for even the quietest to contribute. If you need ideas, visit Google's re:Work site (ReWork. WithGoogle.com) where they share best practices from their study.

If you need any more evidence, psychological safety also creates two more powerful effects. First, it allows for vulnerability. Dr. Brené Brown is most known for her research on shame and vulnerability at the University of Houston. Both of her TED talks are the most viewed in history. She states, "Let me go on the record and say that vulnerability is the birthplace of innovation, creativity and change." Second, psychological safety builds trust and camaraderie, two of the three core components of organizations that make the "Great Place to Work" list (the third is pride). If you want to unleash the real potential of your travelers, make psychological safety a priority.

Empower Social Connections

Camaraderie is a measure of social connection. We are wired to be social creatures. Entire segments of our biology are dedicated to forming meaningful bonds with others and as we learned in section II, change can often impact the social maps built by the entorhinal cortex. In addition, the amygdala is more reactive around unfamiliar people, who can be perceived as potential threats. It's vital to support your travelers in building social connections and camaraderie with each other as quickly as possible. And it will pay off on several fronts.

Some people scoff at team building, and I certainly have experienced my share of cheesy games. But when done right, team building is a powerful tool for building rapport, trust, and positive relationships. It can also begin a culture of psychological safety, and even protect people from pain as we are biologically attuned to our social status. Dr. Naomi Eisenberger, a professor at UCLA, studies this phenomenon and states, "Our research has shown that feeling socially excluded activates some of the same neural regions that are activated in response to physical pain." She goes on to explain that in the workplace, this reaction can be triggered by several common experiences:

- Being ignored
- Perceiving that you are being excluded from a group
- Rejection
- Starting work with a new team
- Being alone among strangers
- Working in culture other than your own

Needless to say, these are all experiences that can happen during change journeys. As a leader, you need to identify when and where people's social connections are likely to be new, strained, or erased and help build them up as quickly as possible. This might include creating social experiences for the group to get to know each other in a relaxed setting, working together on a subcommittee or task team, or a formal team-building experience. Again, this can be made playful and fun and may even be enhanced through technology and apps. Many companies are now creating lunch meetups and providing fun team activities, like geocaching or game nights, to enhance networking and camaraderie.

Patience. Patience. Patience.

The last, and perhaps most important, tool in your connection kit is patience. Patience is crucial because leading a change journey can be hard work. Not only do you have your own experiences through the change initiative, you are now responsible for your travelers' experiences and success. You need to provide stability and guidance while expressing empathy and support. And sometimes your travelers will not show you the appreciation you deserve and they might even be snarky or grumpy.

Patience will be a tool that you use every day, particularly when you approach the peak of your change journey, and also near the end when everyone is running out of steam. Find ways to stay grounded and keep your sense of humor. Partner with another leader so you can coach and support each other, even commiserating when you need. And use the strategies from Chapter 16.

Change Done Right: Three Case Studies

To see some of these principles in action, let's look at three successful change initiatives.

University of California: Merging Services in a Time of Budget Cuts

As a result of an ongoing state fiscal shortfall, the University of California experienced drastic cuts to its annual operating budget, which forced reductions at each of the ten campuses. To meet the goals at the Santa Barbara campus, the Division of Student Affairs needed to make unprecedented changes to the services it offered while maintaining quality support to the 20,000 enrolled students. In addition, it needed to move several departments into one building, combining staffs and services where possible. Anxiety was high as people worried about layoffs.

While this could have been a time when departments competed against each other for meager resources, the executive leaders of the division decided to create an opportunity for enhanced collaboration. They first established some guiding values that became widely known by all of the employees. These were printed on posters, discussed in meetings, and people were recognized for living them.

Next, they empowered the directors to engage in joint problem-solving of how best to use the total building space and budget allotted, no longer "owning" a certain piece of it. To make the process safe, the executives made a guarantee that everyone would keep their jobs but now there were opportunities to innovate new roles, programs, and ways of working.

Directors then empowered employees to problem-solve specific challenges through cross-functional project groups. As a result, people made new social connections and built rapport, which led to new ideas for collaborations.

Every stage of the process was celebrated with group gatherings that featured humor, recognition, and ice cream. While the process was hard work, employees were positive, engaged, and ultimately created a new way of working that kept everyone employed and delivered better services more effectively.

Microsoft: Maximizing Global Resources
As this software giant grew, it built a global workforce in over 100 different countries representing nearly as many languages and cultures. Over time, software development teams were operating in as many as four different timezones, making true collaboration difficult. As a result, it was taking longer to get products and features out the door in a timely manner, which impacted the customer experience.

Executive leaders empowered the directors to solve this problem. The directors met and identified a few clear objectives: (1) increase speed to market, (2) create a way to better partner across geographies, and (3) develop clear measurements of success.

Then they took a deep dive into the data together, learning the current state of the teams, and identifying the bottlenecks and assumptions that were driving current practices. They were held accountable as a group, which required them to let go of silos and territories and instead take ownership of the greater good of the customers and the company.

Together, they designed and implemented several solutions. Teams were reconfigured to better align with geographies and time zones. They developed a strategy that took advantage of where the best tech talent already existed, using it to shape key hiring initiatives and some targeted acquisitions. They also created a scorecord that rated teams on collaboration, leadership, and efficiency. All of these efforts led to faster time-to-market and increased customer satisfaction.

Boeing: Innovating a New Training Model
Boeing was already in the business of building exceptional aircraft and training the pilots who flew them and mechanics who maintained them. An opportunity arose to partner with Berkshire-Hathaway to separate the flight training school and create a new subsidiary that would offer global training to flight crews around the world.

The 400-person team was well ensconced within Boeing's current culture, which is known for its precision and adherence to high standards. Yet, innovating a new model meant that the employees would need to embrace a spirit of entrepreneurship that focused on the customer experience in a whole new way.

The leaders knew this could create anxiety among the team who might worry that "new" meant displacing jobs. So instead of focusing on building a new training model, they homed in on the question "How do we make the customer experience even better?"

To create safety and build rapport, the leaders interviewed every single employee, asking for their sincere input. They asked employees about what was working, strengths that could be leveraged, and opportunities to build something better. Using that information, the leaders crafted a "go forward" plan that allowed the group to honor their past and then collectively create "the new us."

The senior leaders also executed a well-designed communication plan that provided consistent and transparent information. At every stage, employees would find new materials on their desks, like relevant books or stickers with the new mission statement and values, that supported the shift to a new culture and way of working.

Employees were provided with extensive training on integrated leadership, customer satisfaction, new methods in instructional design, and collaboration, all of which supported their ultimate success.

As you can see in these case studies, people in the leader roles can enable and empower travelers to move through a change journey successfully, no matter how steep it is.

18. The Guide's Process

Change journeys are very much like the real treks and hikes I use metaphorically throughout this book. Yet I am amazed how many guides embark on a change journey without the proper preparation or plan. It's like going on a hike up Mount Fuji without training beforehand and leaving your hiking boots and sleeping bag at home. You might get up the mountain but it's unlikely that you will get back home again alive. No wonder so many change initiatives don't make it.

The guide's process is crucial to the success of the change journey and the goal is to get all your travelers up and over the peak and back down safely and, hopefully, happy. Using the tools we discussed in the last chapter—navigation, motivation and connection—in varying degrees as needed will support your efforts.

Here's an overview of the guide's process:
- Preparing for the journey
- Readying the travelers
- Starting on the journey (resistance phase)
- Approaching the peak (resignation phase)
- Gathering momentum (embracement phase)
- Seeing the finish line (engagement phase)
- Dealing with the unexpected

Preparing for the Journey

The success of your change journey will directly reflect your preparation. For the small, quick changes (the pebble on the trail), preparation will be minimal. But for the other three types of change journeys (the long, steady trek; the quick hike up a steep hill; and the long, intense climb), preparation is crucial to your success. This might seem obvious but preparation needs to come *before* you start the actual change. Your travelers will be relying on you and if you're winging it, it's going to add to their distress rather than decrease it, activating parts of the brain that are not helpful for your overall goals.

Do what you need to feel so solid in your plan that you exude calmness and confidence. If you have ever taken a sporting lesson, or done any kind of guided tour, you know how important this is. If your leader seems scattered or rushed, it can freak you out. You need them to know what they are doing and make you feel like you can do it too.

There is actually a biological source for this. Within the brain, we have mirror neurons that fire in our brains as we watch another person do an activity or feel an emotion. Neuroscientists like Dr. Giacomo Rizzolatti from the University of Parma and Dr. Marco Iacoboni at UCLA have discovered that mirror neurons play a vital role in how we learn, how we understand another's intentions, and how we feel empathy. When you see someone under stress, your "stress-feeling" mirror neurons fire up too, creating a sensation in your own brain for stress. And the reverse is true—when you see someone looking calm and confident, it lights up calmness and confidence in your own brain.

As a guide, your moods, words, and actions have a profound impact on travelers. So take the time to prepare yourself for the journey. Make sure you understand the why of the change and all the elements of the change plan. Test drive the elements of the change plan and practice your messaging. If parts are not clear, ask questions. If you think something is not going to work, speak up. And if you need more support, request it. Remember, the goal is to naturally exude calmness and confidence because you are genuinely prepared and ready to lead.

Another aspect of preparation is setting up the route. It should be ready for the travelers so that once they begin on the journey they can easily make their way through without stumbling unnecessarily. Many people think that change initiatives fail due to big and unforeseen circumstances. Yet the truth is that most fail for little reasons—things that easily could have been avoided or addressed if someone had done a better job of setting up the route in advance.

Everyone expects careful route preparation when people are riding in the Tour de France or attempting to summit Mount Everest. Long before the travelers actually arrive, mileage is calculated, maps are created, signs are hung, and stations for water, rest, and food are set up. The amount of support needed correlates with the physical exertion required and the length of the journey. For example, food and water stations are placed more frequently for a marathon than for a charity walk. For the California AIDS Ride, we had sleeping quarters, shower trucks, medical stations, and even entertainment spaced out and set up so that the riders were supported for success from the opening bell until the last rider crossed the finish line seven days and 550 miles later.

For workplace changes, this might translate to things like this:
- Detailed action plans and timelines
- Signs and posters with key messages

- Websites and apps
- Large- and small-group communications, like emails and all-hands meetings
- Meeting agendas
- Training (in-person sessions, online videos, documentation)
- Coaching
- Recognition, rewards, and celebrations

Ideally, other leaders in your organization are thinking these things through and the change journey reflects thoughtful planning and the right level of support. If so, you just need to do your part and make sure you guide your group of travelers through the journey. You'll be most confident if you run the route ahead of them, making sure everything is ready. And then come back and lead with confidence. Or, if you discover that the right planning and support is not yet in place, speak up! Your preparation might just be the thing that triggers a better change journey for everyone.

And don't be bound by what is provided to you. If it's lacking, innovate some solutions. You can easily create your own maps and signs and support stations. You might even empower some of your travelers to help you do this. Pick your stronger and more experienced folks to be a scouting team, thinking a few steps ahead on the journey. This turns it in to a problem-solving experience for them and also takes some of the workload off of you.

Finally, preparation includes getting yourself ready for journey too. You will also be taking the change journey in addition to the workload of leading, coaching, and troubleshooting. You will need emotional intelligence to manage the various challenging feelings that will arise and patience for the process.

Think about what helps you feel calm and grounded and do more of those things. Dial up your self-care, making sure you get plenty of sleep and good nutrition. And if you have not explored the benefits of mindfulness, I recommend that you do.

Readying the Travelers

Another key element of preparation is readying your travelers. Before you head off on the trek, take a look at your group. What kind of shape are they in? Assess their motivation for this journey. Do you have people who will be running toward the change with enthusiasm and energy? Do you have a few who will be actively digging in their heels? It just doesn't make sense to ignore their motivation because it will actively impact the group every day.

You can also assess if they are carrying a heavy load that needs to be accounted for. Separate from our motivation, aspects of our personal lives also impact our ability to move easily through change. For example, an employee who is working through an illness or injury is likely to have less energy. As would a new parent who is in the throes of sleepless nights and overwhelm.

I think of these things as rocks in a backpack. I can't necessarily remove them but it helps to know who is under extra stress and carrying a heavier load than others. And if there is anything I can do to help lighten that load, I try. Sometimes, small shifts to projects, working hours, or resources can make all the difference. This is where you can also employ the buddy system. If people are paired up or put in small teams, they can help each other. If you do this, make sure that your people with heavy backpacks are paired with folks who have bandwidth to spare.

After you assess your team, consider what you can do to get them ready. For real hikes and treks, people train to build up their physical strength. They work out and practice and stretch. What does that look like for a workplace change? Perhaps helping them learn some time-management skills now will really pay off when you are getting close to the peak of the mountain. Perhaps doing some trust and rapport-building now will help them lean on each other when they are getting tired and frustrated. Perhaps encouraging people to take some downtime now and rest up will payoff tenfold in just a few weeks.

Consider the skills, habits, and relationships they will need to succeed and start building those now, before you start on the trail. And, when possible, let your team know about the journey ahead of time. If they know the destination, route, and timeline, they can become active participations in their own preparation, even innovating solutions that increase the success of your whole group.

Starting on the Journey: Resistance Phase

Starting out on the trail, keep some things in mind as you guide people through these early stages. (Just a reminder: we don't really have to worry about resistance with pebbles on the trail, the "green zone" changes. But for the other three journeys, be mindful of these key phases.) Usually, the beginning of the journey is when we will hit some resistance. Humans are wired to resist change so no matter how great of a job you have done getting ready, grumbling will still happen. They will question the change, focus on potential losses, and likely have strong emotions, especially if it's a steeper journey or if they are moving through several change journeys simultaneously.

Your best strategy is to communicate early and often, being as transparent as possible. Share the why, how, and when and treat your travelers as participants. If there is any part of the experience they can design, let them. This works so much better than when the leaders, trailblazers, and guides do it all. In fact, studies show that when people choose for themselves, they are far more committed to the outcome, by a factor of five to one. If they cannot choose the change, then let them choose as many aspects of their change journey as possible.

Some possibilities to consider:

- Creating a map and updating progress in a way that's visible to the team
- Identifying key milestones and designing the celebration events
- Creating meaningful rewards
- Building a sense of team identity, perhaps a team name or mascot
- Creating an agreed-upon way of handling conflict
- Gamifying the experience—can it be done faster or better?
- Designing ways to include self-care, mindfulness, and play into the journey
- To be determined (let them figure out what they want and need)

When they grumble, listen. And listen carefully, as they are likely sharing their worries about what they might lose. The more you know their fears, the better you can allay them. It's very common for people to worry about the issues we have already discussed like autonomy, mastery, and purpose as well as status, certainty, relatedness, and fairness. In her book *Rising Strong*, Dr. Brené Brown, says that during times of change, people have a fear of irrelevance. We all want to matter and we all want to be seen and heard.

So, see them and hear them. Let them know they matter. That doesn't mean making false promises but having empathy for their concerns will go a long way to helping them through the psychological transition. And it will build trust and rapport.

I always remind leaders and guides that the travelers' grumbling is not a reflection of leadership, it's just people being human. Modeling patience and empathy will go a long way to helping the group feel safer and calmer.

Provide consistent and reliable guidance, exuding calmness and confidence. Now is the time when you get them to trust the guide rope you are building so they can hold on to it during difficult moments.

Approaching the Peak: Resignation Phase

At this phase, you have made it through the initial grumbling but as the climb gets steeper or takes a very long time, people may get frustrated and even depressed. They have not yet hit the peak where they see the potential benefits, so it can be helpful to remind people of the why and all the good things that are coming.

Your leadership at this stage is crucial and yet it can't be so out of step with their emotions that you seem insensitive or clueless. I recommend having a meeting or celebration that acknowledges how far they have already come. Recognize people and have them recognize each other, and find a way to do it that matches the tone of your group. If they are into silly, do silly. If they are more serious, do serious. If you are not sure, ask them.

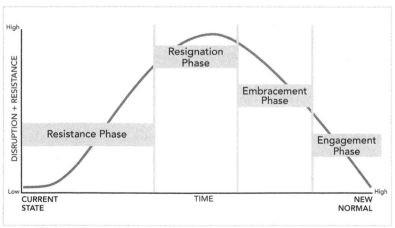

The phases of the change journey

This is a great time to ask people to share stories of what is working. These stories can be what's working with the change. Or what's working with how they are moving forward during a difficult journey. Or even how they have overcome an obstacle. Shine the light on all the good stuff you can find to enliven the group and create a positive experience for the brain.

This is actually a form of appreciative inquiry, a method that naturally brings out in the best in a group through a collaborative process. After you celebrate, let them know that they are getting close to the peak and ask what they need for this next push. Have them own their journey and brainstorm what would help them. Then do your best to provide it. You may also need a boost at this stage so consider meeting up with other guides and support each other and celebrate your successes too.

And always, be that steady and calm presence, that strong guide rope they can hold onto as they keep moving forward.

Gathering Momentum: Embracement Phase

By this time, you have gotten over the hump of resistance, which feels good but don't let down your guard. This is still a very vulnerable phase so you want to tend to the momentum as it continues to build.

Keep being the calm, steady presence, sharing the why and how of the journey. At this stage people often have a lot of questions, things you have likely already talked about. But since they have now psychologically gotten on board, they will have a new interest in what this change is for, how it's going to get done, and they may be ready to add their own ideas and suggestions.

Leaders and guides might get a little frustrated here because it's going to feel like people weren't paying attention to all the great communicating you have been doing. Breathe and dial up your patience. Remember, they're just being human. And it's really a positive sign, because the questions are evidence that they have made the turn and are now looking toward potential gains. Listen and respond. And don't worry that revisiting these topics will cause the group to backslide. In fact, this is a great time to listen even more attentively because they will often see issues that need to be addressed or have ideas that should be implemented. Some of the best innovations come at this stage of a change journey but only if the guides listen.

This is also the phase when you are likely to start implementing new behaviors. Be sure you use trainings to get those repetitions built. This is when people are likely to fail so create an atmosphere where it's okay to make mistakes and harvest the learning from those mishaps.

Somewhere near the end of this phase, have another celebratory gathering, recognizing people and calling out all the good work they did at getting on board and moving forward. This helps the brain see another positive reward in change.

Seeing the Finish Line: Engagement Phase

By this phase, you might feel like you are done but you are not, so resist the temptation to turn your attention to other things. While your travelers are on board and gaining speed, keep the guide rope in place and make sure they complete the journey. During mountain climbing and physical treks, this is the most dangerous part of the expedition. Because the hard part is over, people can lose focus and take unnecessary risks, especially because the fatigue of the exertion is setting in. Sadly, most deaths in mountain climbing occur after people have summited and are heading back down.

You can certainly take on an air of celebration but keep your calm and steady presence in place. This is a great time to reorient people toward the finish line. Be clear on what it means to complete the change initiative and which metrics matter. Many change initiatives actually fail at this stage because they don't reach completion. Leaders erroneously assume that since the group is "this close" they will naturally keep on going.

But the reality is that by this point, the team has been tasked with other changes and has started on other journeys. And because this one seems "in the bag," the guides head to other treks and the trailblazers start packing up, which both threaten the success of the journey and denies the travelers the satisfaction of the final celebration. The brain needs that sense of completion to code change as a success. And if it falls apart at this stage, the organization will have invested time and money in something that did not succeed, and the travelers will be marked with a failure despite the great work they did. So, keep guiding until the last traveler crosses the finish line and the change journey is officially over.

Then formally close out the experience for people. Don't let it become something that never gets scheduled because it's an important element of the brain science of change. If there were failures and chal lenges, that is okay. Learning is an important part of how we improve, so have a meeting where you talk through what happened and what should have shifted. I recommend that you have a post-mortem meeting assessing the change and the outcomes. And a separate event to celebrate the journey and the travelers.

A note about celebrations. Celebrations can come in all kinds of forms from the casual break (think pizza party, shooting pool, or silent disco) to an offsite adventure (like bowling, geocaching, or glassblowing) to the elaborate and expensive (awards dinner or trip to Vegas or Hawaii). The most important quality is that they align with the culture and context of your travelers. Some of the most cringe-worthy scenes from TV shows like *The Office* or *Superstore* are when the boss is "celebrating" the team in a way that totally misses the mark. This is why I recommend that you ask your travelers to design the rewards and celebrations, because then you will know it will be right. Give them a budget and let them create what will make them feel honored.

Dealing with the Unexpected: Roadblocks, Storms, and Landslides—Oh My!

In reality, few (if any) change journeys roll along as planned. Even when the expedition designers, trailblazers, guides, and travelers all do a phenomenal job, unexpected things happen. And the best change leaders plan for the unexpected.

With the Change Journey model, you'll have already accounted for typical issues, like what's to be expected when taking a highly resistant group on a long, steep climb journey. Or having a group of travelers who don't have the skills they need to be successful on the trail ahead of them. The model allows you to assess and predict, which will help your expectations become more accurate. And the strategies I laid out in the previous section should help you address many potential issues. However, unexpected challenges often come from unanticipated sources and they may threaten the success of the entire change journey or the success of a group of travelers. I have observed that they seem to fall into three categories and your response to each should be a little different because the damage they do varies as well.

Roadblocks

Sometimes something drops onto the trail that prevents your travelers from moving forward until it's addressed. Roadblocks don't affect the overall change journey, so the goal and path remain the same, but you will still need to respond to the roadblock, possibly climbing over it or taking a short detour.

A roadblock's impact depends on your team and timeline as well as the size of the obstacle. I think of it as a boulder on the trail. Experienced travelers who are highly motivated for the journey might handle it before you even know it happened. If the block is large, they may need to stop and strategize the best solution for getting over or around it. But a roadblock may completely demoralize highly resistant travelers or those carrying heavy backpacks, causing them to backslide into some negative emotions. Depending on how long it takes to resolve, a roadblock can also impact the timeline, either pushing it out so the journey takes longer, or forcing a steeper incline.

Here are some examples of roadblocks:

- A supplier is delayed in delivering a component
- The cost of a necessary resource just increased
- Another team's process or product is not yet finished
- A key player or guide leaves the team or company
- A regional difference has not been accounted for
- A trailblazer did not adequately prepare a necessary resource

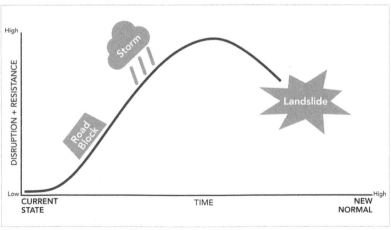

Types of unexpected challenges

As the guide, you'll want to be a calm and steady presence. If you spot the roadblock on the horizon, the sooner you tell your team the better. If your team suspects you withheld information, it can harm your rapport with the group.

My favorite way to handle a roadblock is to turn it into a problem-solving challenge. Have your travelers take the lead on finding the best solution as they are likely to have great ideas and will feel more empowered if they are taking the lead. Once you get through the roadblock, celebrate the success and teamwork.

Storms

The second type of unexpected challenge is like a blizzard or sandstorm. Storms are something that come from the outside and descend upon the journey and travelers. Again, the parameters of the change journey don't change but the storm definitely affects the timeline because your travelers will need to hunker down and wait it out. The difference between a storm and a roadblock is time—storms take longer to resolve, so they tend to stop the group's forward momentum. A roadblock can turn into a storm if it becomes and long and drawn out process.

Examples of storms:
- A new policy or regulation goes into effect that needs to be addressed by the designers/leaders
- A person or group raises concerns about the change that needs to be resolved by the designers/leaders
- A process or technology is not configured correctly and will take time to fix
- A shift occurs in the market but is likely to right itself in the near future
- A designer/leader makes a significant change that needs to be worked through

When a storm hits, remain the calm and steady presence, talking them through it. As mentioned, the sooner you can let them know a storm is on the way, the better. Your value as a guide will be less impressive if you come bounding up announcing the storm when they are already buried under two feet of snow. Giving them warning helps them physically and mentally prepare.

The impact of the storm on your group really depends on how you handle it. The shared experience might bind your travelers together, but it's not unusual for added anxiety and strife to divide a group.

Obviously, the former is preferred. Be transparent about what you know and how long you anticipate the storm to last, and address how this delay impacts them and whether it affects how their performance will be viewed. The amygdala is going to create anxiety about this change within a change. And the habenula might cause more concern about failure and blame. There is nothing more stressful to a group than to be prevented from being successful but still held accountable for the result. You will likely hear a lot of questions and comments to that effect so come prepared with the answers.

Luckily, you are unlikely to be on the side of a real mountain building an igloo to withstand a snowstorm. So your travelers can probably use the storm as a break in this particular journey to focus on their other work, especially since they may be on other journeys too. It might be good to help them figure out how to best use their time and energy until the storm passes.

When things start up again, reconvene the group to tell them what caused the storm (if they don't already know), adjusting the map and timeline accordingly. If a long time has passed, you may need to reorient them to the goal and assess their overall motivation since things might have shifted in the interim. Reestablish your guide rope, mark where you are on the route, and get them started. Don't expect them to just pop right back to where they were before. They likely need to warm up and build some momentum again. If you can, acknowledge and celebrate their adaptability.

Landslides
The final type of unexpected challenge completely wipes your group off the mountain, creating a sudden end to the change journey. These are significant shifts in the landscape that will not only affect this change journey but likely several other things about your work environment.

Some examples of landslides:
- The financial collapse of your organization
- A merger or acquisition
- An election, lawsuit, or regulation
- A natural or geopolitical disaster

Landslides are the most disorienting because they create sudden, seismic shifts so your travelers will likely be stunned. They put an obvious end to this particular change journey, and launch a whole new one.

Because your travelers are likely experiencing confusion and shock, it's helpful to bring them together and maintain your role as guide. Help them understand and process this shift and allow them to ask questions. You can leverage the team's connection and your time together to create some stability around the new, bigger change that caused the landslide.

It might be helpful to share the why, if you know it, and help them see the route or map. If you don't know or can't share, let them know that more information will be coming soon and ask them to have patience. Remind them that this might be a good time to use the troika of self-care, mindfulness, and play and, if possible, organize some in-office options at work (e.g., games, meditation class, potluck) to take people's minds off the unknowns. And still end with recognizing and celebrating the team's accomplishments for the original change journey.

Your Learning Journey

To help you thrive through upcoming change journeys, apply these tools to create your own personal change success plan:

- Do your inventory of the change. Capture key insights.
- Identify ways you can increase your self-care, engage in mindfulness practices, and schedule time for play.
- Explore the ten options for being an active participant. Identify some specific actions you can take in the coming weeks to help yourself succeed.
- Whether you are a traveler or a guide, explore the tools for navigation, motivation, and connection. Identify a few tools from each category that would be helpful to you. Clarify how you could create or use them.
- Since psychological safety is so crucial to every group's success, identify a few ways you can help build more psychological safety with your team/colleagues.
- Whether you are a traveler or a guide, explore the guide's process. Identify a few strategies from each phase that would be helpful to you. Explain how you could create or use them.

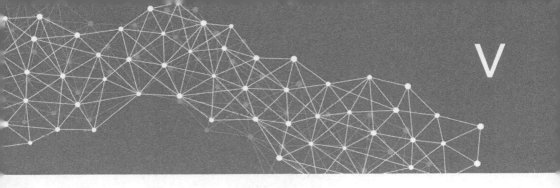

THE PATH AHEAD:
ORGANIZATIONAL GROWTH
+ CONSCIOUSNESS

19. Organization Growth: The Greiner Curve

Change may feel relentless and chaotic, but there is a method in the madness. In all my years of consulting, I started seeing the same issues over and over, even though I was working with different industries and sectors. The same challenges cropped up and the solutions were similar too. Much like Bill Murray in the movie *Groundhog Day*, I could eerily predict what was coming and when.

This is because organizations grow and change in predictable ways, moving through stages of development and levels of consciousness. Each shift brings a host of predictable changes as the organization seeks to resolve common issues of growth. Lots of scholars have studied organization growth and development and I have found this information invaluable in my consulting work.

My favorite model for organizational growth is the Greiner Curve. Identifying your organization's stage of development and, more importantly, the stage it is growing into will help you anticipate the changes coming your way. In his research, Dr. Larry Greiner, a professor at USC's Marshall School of Business, has identified that organizations move through six distinct phases that are a function of its age and size. But organizations move through the phases at radically different paces. For example, a large, traditional financial institution will have a much slower and gentler progression than a fast-growing tech start-up. The time in each phase can range from months to decades—the speed is dictated by how quickly you are hiring and adding more employees, thus making your organization bigger.

Every stage of growth ultimately leads to a crisis point when the current structure can no longer support what the organization needs to grow, and these crisis points force change, transforming the organization to the next phase. The organization can then experience a period of relative stability until it hits the next crisis point. These periods of stability can range from months to decades but, inevitably, growth in size will push it to the next crisis point and transformation.

As I describe the six phases, see if you can identify your organization's current position on the curve.

Phase One: Growth Through Creativity
This is when the founders build the organization. The organization is small so people wear many hats and communication is spontaneous

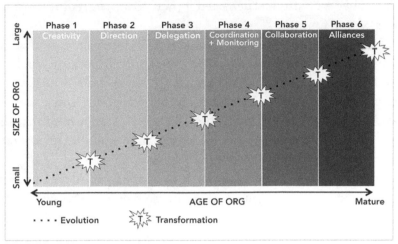

The Greiner Curve

and informal. People know each other and work closely together, which usually creates high amounts of trust and psychological safety, and sometimes playfulness and fun. Since the small group is pushing for and designing the changes as well as implementing them, there is little resistance to, and high motivation for, change. This team moves fast to solve issues and hierarchical decision-making rarely exists. This is a very creative time when there are fast failures and quick wins. Formal processes don't exist.

As the organization gets bigger and adds more employees to handle its growing success, it leads to the crisis point of leadership, where professional management needs to be brought in to help run the various functions like finance, marketing, and human resources. The needs of the organization have grown past what the original group can provide. Psychologically, this original team may be disappointed that things are beginning to feel quite different. The safe feeling of a small, intimate family may start to shift.

Phase Two: Growth Through Direction
Additional leaders are brought in to manage various functions. You are likely to see a lot of change pushed down within functions as each leader attempts to bring their part of the house in order and prepare it for future growth.

This can be a tender time for legacy employees who have been there from the start as they likely had ideas about what changes were needed. They may also feel demoted if they no longer report to, or have the ear of, the founders.

These new leaders tend to hire people that they have worked with before, which has its advantages but can also strain existing relationships. Since the organization is still fairly small, leaders believe that change initiatives can be launched quickly, especially since they may feel an urgency to "whip things into shape." It is important that these leaders are sensitive and focus on augmenting and enhancing rather than constantly pointing out what is broken.

Simultaneously, the organization is focusing on developing new products and services to gain enough market share to be viable in the long run. The original team is likely to protect what they built, even if it isn't scalable and may be reluctant to diversify their products and services. At some point, again months to decades later, the scale of the offerings get too big for the leaders to monitor, which creates the crisis point of autonomy where work and authority need to be delegated to others.

Phase Three: Growth Through Delegation
That leads to the third phase, where layers of hierarchy are added and authority is delegated down. Roles start to be segmented into levels like senior director, director, and assistant director. Top management become less involved in the day-to-day details and turns their focus to the organization's long-term strategy—at least, that's the goal. But early in this phase, it can be rather messy as new leaders may not yet be ready to take the reins, or the top leaders are reluctant to let go and may micromanage their functions. The top leaders may need to shift into smaller roles or out of the organization as the growth and needs of the company often outpace their current capabilities and leadership skills.

Changes during this phase include all kinds of organization redesigns and changes in reporting structures. This drives changes in many of the administrative support functions like finance, HR, facilities, and technology to keep pace with the expansion of employees. Eventually, things smooth out and the organization settles into some stability.

Over time, the sheer size of an organization starts to stress the current policies and channels of communication, creating the crisis point of control, where the different parts of the organization need to work together better.

Phase Four: Growth Through Coordination and Monitoring
This ushers in the fourth phase, where new policies and procedures are introduced to bring structure to the various parts of the organization and consistency across it. Changes include the creation of company-wide practices in managing teams, performance reviews, financial practices like budgeting and spending, and the transition to formal processes, shared technology systems, and platforms.

At first, this effort helps bring stability and consistency to the organization's broader scope. You might be gaining some efficiency and economies of scale, and many problem areas, like inequities in performance reviews, are addressed. But people might also start to feel that things are too rigid or "corporate" and many employees leave at this stage, preferring to find organizations that are still in phases two or three, which in turn changes the makeup of teams and reporting relationships.

While policies are good at first, organizations often over-compensate and begin to create policies for the "lowest common denominator." For example, while 98 percent of the employees show up to work on time and use the corporate credit card appropriately, the company will react to the behavior of a few bozos who made bad choices by creating overly restrictive policies. All of this combined leads to the inevitable crisis point of red tape, where bureaucracy gets burdensome.

Phase Five: Growth Through Collaboration
To solve this problem, the organization has to switch gears and move to the fifth phase of growth through collaboration. Bureaucracy is replaced by a range of scalable and agile systems that support more flexibility. Instead of a rigid system for making decisions, emotionally intelligent leaders are trusted to use good judgment.

This phase requires a change of top leaders who can work in this more organic and fluid way. Naturally, this drives all kinds of new changes in philosophy and style as well as organizational structure. Since this is a fairly dramatic shift from the previous stage, it ushers in a lot of new changes, but they are often undoing or redoing changes that employees had already moved through. Again, an organization can spend months to years in this phase but, as it grows, it eventually arrives at the crisis point of internal growth, where the organization must look outside itself for new growth opportunities.

In the final phase the organization can only solve its challenges by partnering with other organizations, through actions like outsourcing, mergers, franchises, etc. These actions bring a whole new range of changes as complex entities try to integrate products, leadership styles, values, and cultures (not to mention policies, email systems, currencies, and regulations). Top executives (and their legal teams) broker most ventures of this nature, which are kept secret until they are announced, much to the surprise of the employees. While they make take months or years to unfold, they often suddenly drive countless changes and psychological reactions.

This expansion ultimately creates some dilution as various entities mix and merge together. Over time, this leads to the crisis point of identity, where the organization must refocus on its vision, mission, and strategy and revise it into a unified whole.

It's important to note that while the model appears linear, organizations can slide back into previous phases. It is not uncommon to be on the edge between two stages. It is also common that the core part of the business is more developed and in a different stage than newer functions.

So, have you identified your organization's phase on the model? More importantly, can you tell what crisis point and transformation is coming? When I consult with leaders, I ask them to identify the overall phase as well as the phases for each of the functions as this can provide valuable information for understanding change. It helps them predict the next crisis point so they can prepare rather than just react. All kinds of troubling situations can be avoided with thoughtful and planned preparation.

As you become more familiar with the phases of organizational growth, you can begin to realize that change initiatives are a natural output of development. How work gets done, what work gets done and who does the work shifts significantly through each phase, which requires precise interventions. While our brains may be wired to want static and predictable companies, organizations are organic things, living ecosystems that shift and move. I use the Greiner Curve to help everyone embrace the fact that change is constant and even somewhat predictable.

20. Organizational Consciousness: Becoming Teal

While the Greiner Curve is a great model for organizational growth, another driver of change in organizations is the evolution of consciousness. Frederic Laloux has been researching this topic and reveals some very interesting developments in his book *Reinventing Organizations: A Guide to Creating Organizations Inspired by the Next Stage of Human Consciousness*. You may have heard of him because Tony Hsieh, the CEO of Zappos, is using Laloux's work to intentionally shift the consciousness of his company.

Scholars studying human consciousness from many disciplines—neuroscientists, biologists, psychologists, sociologists, and even anthropologists—have found it develops through stages. Laloux discovered that organizational development maps to these stages of human consciousness, and as humans evolve, so do the organizations they build.

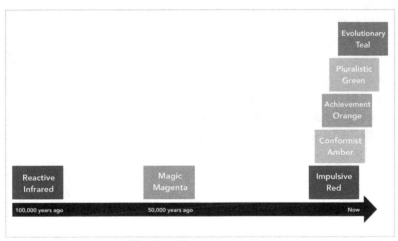

Timeline of human consciousness

Like Greiner's model, human consciousness evolves in sudden transformations. We have currently entered a unique time, when consciousness is evolving more quickly with five levels of consciousness actively shaping organizations over the past 200 years. Laloux states, "Every transition to a new stage of consciousness has ushered in a whole new era in human history. At every juncture, everything changed: society, the economy, the power structures…and organizational models." Laloux goes on to explain each of the organizational stages, each with a corresponding color, starting with Infrared and Magenta, and ending with Teal, the latest level that is becoming visible now.

Lest you think Laloux is out in left field, he is one of a number of people who are talking about the intersection of consciousness and business. Whole Foods CEO John Mackey partnered with Raj Sisodia to write *Conscious Capitalism*. Dr. Fred Kofman wrote *Conscious Business* and now consults with companies and governments around the world to bring conscious practices to the forefront. And it's not just a feel-good exercise. Companies operating in the green and teal levels of consciousness significantly outperform the others, according to *Firms of Endearment: How World Class Companies Profit from Passion and Purpose* (by Rajendra Sisodia, David Wolfe, and Jagdish Sheth), which details a powerful study of over 65 companies, comparing them to the companies featured in James Collins's bestselling book *Good to Great*. They found that Firms of Endearment companies outperformed the others by over 1,400 percent!

I have seen clear evidence of this conscious evolution in organizations and it is at the heart of many change initiatives as well as shifts in what employees want and what drives engagement.

In every place I have ever worked, whether employee or consultant, I have seen evidence supporting Laloux's model, so I consider it an essential tool when assessing organizations. I will provide a quick summary here but I strongly recommend you read his book and view some of the videos and resources he has posted on his website ReinventingOrganizations.com. His rich research and detailed descriptions really helped me use this model in my work.

It's important to remember that no stage is "better" or "worse" than another. In fact, Nick Petrie from the Center of Creative Leadership states, "There is nothing inherently 'better' about being at a higher level of development, just as an adolescent is not 'better' than a toddler. Any level of development is okay; the question is whether that level of development is a good fit for the task at hand."

Red/Impulsive

These organizations thrive in chaotic environments like times of war or when competition for resources is high. These organizations are highly reactive and have a short-term focus. The constant exercise of power by the leader keeps people in line, and fear is the primary tool for control. The key breakthroughs of this stage are division of labor and command authority. Current examples in today's society include the mafia, tribal militias, and street gangs. Media headlines about events in Syria and

Venezuela show that this consciousness is expressed in times of intense survival.

Amber/Conformist

These organizations use top-down command and control as well as highly formal roles within a hierarchical pyramid. The goal is stability and consistency, which are often crucial to the organization's success. Leaders determine the what and how of the organization and members are expected to execute as instructed. Stability is achieved through rigorous processes and zero-tolerance for nonconformity. The core breakthroughs of this phase are formal roles, scalable hierarchies, and long-term processes. Current examples include military and law enforcement as well as public school systems and the Catholic Church.

	RED Impulsive	AMBER Conformist	ORANGE Achievement	GREEN Pluralistic	TEAL Evolutionary
Description	Thrives in chaos. Constant exercise of power by leader. Control through fear. Highly reactive and short-term.	Highly formal hierarchical roles. Command and control from top. Stability through rigorous process.	Focus is on profit, competition, and growth. Innovation is key. Management by objectives.	Within classic pyramid, focus is on culture, values, and employee engagement.	Organization is living system. Focus is on moving to integrated wholeness and authenticity.
Key Breakthroughs	Division of labor Command authority	Formal roles Rigorous processes	Innovation Accountability Meritocracy	Empowerment Values culture Stakeholders	Self-management Wholeness Evolutionary purpose
Guiding Metaphor	Wolf pack	Army	Machine	Family	Living organism
Current Examples	Mafia Tribal militias Street gangs	Military Most government agencies Public schools Catholic Church	Multinational companies Charter schools	Culture-driven organizations (e.g., Southwest, Ben & Jerry's, Google)	Consciousness-driven orgs (e.g., Patagonia, Favi, Morning Star, AES, Sounds True)
"Good" decisions judged by...	Achieving leader's desires	Conforming to social norms	Effectiveness and success Rational and logical	Belonging and harmony People/feeling process	Inner rightness Being of service Rational and intuitive

Conscious evolutiom of organizations

Orange/Achievement

These organizations focus on profit and growth with the goal of beating the competition. Innovation is the key to staying ahead so this stage has driven much of modern capitalism. Leaders use management by objectives (MBOs) or key performance indicators (KPIs) to measure effectiveness and success. Peter Drucker has been a major voice of this stage. Leaders use command and control on what the organization does but middle management has more freedom on how it gets done. The key breakthroughs of this rational/logical approach are accountability, meritocracy, and innovation. Current examples are global companies and charter schools.

Green/Pluralistic

These organizations seek to stay competitive by harnessing extraordinary employee motivation and engagement. Research on the power of employee engagement to drive productivity, customer satisfaction, and retention shows clear evidence of this stage of consciousness. The definition of stakeholder expands beyond shareholders to include customers, employees, and communities. Green organizations focus on creating a great culture through attention to vision and values along with purpose. We often hear through the media about culture-driven organizations like Southwest Airlines, Google, and Ben & Jerry's. For more on the green stage, check out these current bestselling business books:

- *Start Something That Matters* by Blake Mycoskie
- *We First: How Brands and Consumers Use Social Media to Build a Better World* by Simon Mainwaring
- *Delivering Happiness: A Path to Profits, Passion and Purpose* by Tony Hsieh
- *Firms of Endearment: How World-Class Companies Profit from Passion and Purpose* by Rajendra Sisodia, David Wolfe, and Jagdish Sheth
- *Conscious Business: How to Build Value Through Values* by Fred Kofman
- *Conscious Capitalism: Liberating the Heroic Spirit of Business* by John Mackey and Rajendra Sisodia

Teal/Evolutionary

These organizations are just starting to emerge but by no means are they all young start-ups. Laloux features 11 teal organizations in his book ranging in size from 600 to 40,000 employees across a wide range of industries including apparel, manufacturing, technology, and healthcare. He depicts organizations as living systems with a direction of their own that need to be listened to. This shifts the organizational structure from one of hierarchy to more localized and collaborative teams. This shift ushers in new models of decision-making, job responsibilities, and performance management. Known as holacracy, key breakthroughs include self-management, wholeness, and authenticity. Current examples include Patagonia, Morning Star, and AES (a global energy company). Another relevant book is by Brian Robertson, called *Holacracy: The New Management System for a Rapidly Changing World.*

It's important to note that while this is an evolutionary process, some organizations align with a certain stage because it best suits their mission and work. For example, the military will likely always align with the Amber/Conformist stage because it must succeed in often chaotic and dangerous environments where adherence to strict processes is paramount. That doesn't mean that it won't adopt some elements of other stages but its core structure and way of working will stay amber.

In most of today's organizations, I see a blend of orange and green consciousness. Many organizations still set strategic and tactical goals using MBO or KPI terminology and productivity/success is measured in goal achievement. And most modern performance-management systems assess employees against goals, even if they are following the current trend of shifting traditional ratings and annual reviews.

At the same time, organizations are exhibiting quite a few green components as they compete for talent, especially among Millennial and technically trained employees. They create values-driven cultures and focus on employee engagement, often offering all kinds of wonderful perks and benefits. In addition, there is a feeling of "family" within the organization and leaders seek the input of employees and strive to create an environment of employee empowerment.

But it's important to note that there are natural tensions between the orange and green stages, so straddling them is difficult and one inevitably trumps the other. What I see in many organizations is an outward-facing appearance of green elements but with a solidly orange core. Almost like green wrapping paper around an orange box. This can create challenges if employees are drawn to a culture that presents itself as green (often overplayed to draw in good employees) but find that the majority of their experience is ultimately orange. This mismatch often drives turnover and I believe is one of the reasons the average tenure of today's employee is a mere three years.

Clearly, the conscious evolution of organizations drives many change initiatives as the different stages come online. These changes can be sourced in the consciousness of the employees, the leaders, or the customers. We will see elements of orange and green for years to come, with more and more organizations beginning the shift to teal.

There are levels of human consciousness beyond teal including turquoise, indigo, and purple. As more and more humans express those levels, we will see them make their way into human society and organizations decades from now.

Your Learning Journey

Take time to explore how the Greiner Curve and Laloux's model apply to your organization. Consider these questions:

- Which Greiner Curve phase does your organization fall into? What indications do you see?
- Are all functions at the same stage? If not, identify which functions are in which phases.
- What is the next crisis point you will encounter? How can you start preparing now so that you are ready?
- Using Laloux's model, which levels of consciousness does your organization exhibit? Identify how that shows up on a regular basis.
- Are all functions at the same level? If not, can you identify which functions exhibit which levels.
- Think about the senior leaders in your organization. Which consciousness do they each exhibit? How does their consciousness influence the organization?
- Identify which consciousness your top talent exhibits. What are the gaps between their expectations and experiences?
- When you consider these two models and your organization's current state, which changes are likely to unfold over the coming months and years? See if you can look ahead and form some loose predictions.

21. Conclusion: Final Thoughts on Change

No doubt about it: change is the one constant we can count on. It will be part of our professional and personal lives until the moment we take our last breath. And because change in our modern day has become both intense and relentless, our human biology is being pushed to its limits. By leveraging knowledge from neuroscience, biology, and organizational psychology, we can approach change in a new way, understanding our natural resistance and finding ways to help each other thrive through the chaos and confusion.

I hope, as you use the new model and tools I have introduced in this book, you will develop new habits for leading change that directly support your success. You also have the ability to profoundly impact the success of those you lead and influence. Like any skill, practice will increase your competence. Luckily, in today's world, you will have ample opportunities to work with change.

This model has become the centerpiece for manager training at organizations around the world. It is also shaping how leaders design, implement, and track change initiatives across their organizations. I have built a series of training programs, activities, and other tools for people to use when moving through change. Learn more at www.BrittAndreatta.com/Wired-to-Resist.

Consider using this material in your personal life as well. Since I have done this research, my husband and I use the model at home. We share our map of change journeys and our motivation for each one. This has allowed us to better support each other, and also make better decisions around vacations, house projects, and down time.

I'll close by saying that we can all benefit from knowing how to harness our biology to maximize our potential. Continue to tend to your own growth and development. You have a lot of unrealized ability within you—we all do. Part of our journey as humans is learning how to step up to that potential and help others do the same.

Thank you for taking this learning journey with me.

Warmly,

Britt Andreatta

Synthesize Your Learning Journey into Action

As we conclude, look over your notes from the various learning journeys in this book. You should now have a robust understanding of change and how to best navigate its challenges. Take a moment to finalize your notes and create an action plan that will unfold over the next few weeks and months.

- What are your three biggest takeaways from this book?
- What are some actions you can take in the next 30, 60, and 90 days that will help you thrive as a traveler on a change journey?
- If you are in the role of designer, trailblazer or guide for others, what are some actions you can take in the next 30, 60, and 90 days that will help make a better experience for your travelers?
- Consider how you might share some of what you have learned with colleagues and leaders in your organization. For additional resources and training materials to help you with this, visit www.BrittAndreatta.com/Wired-to-Resist.

RESOURCES + REFERENCES

The work of the following scholars, practitioners, and organizations influenced this book.

Articles and Studies

"70% of Hospital Strategic Initiatives Fail: How Hospitals Can Avoid Those Failures" by B. Herman. *Becker's Hospital Review*, 24 Sept 2012.

"A Concept Analysis of Empathy" by T. Wiseman. *Journal of Advanced Nursing*, 1996, Vol. 23: 6.

"A Map for Social Navigation in the Human Brain" by R. Tavares, et al., *Neuron*, 2015, Vol. 87: 1.

"A Theory of Human Motivation" by A. Maslow. *Psychological Review*, 1943, Vol. 50: 4.

"Amygdala—General Considerations" by A. Wright for Department of Neurobiology and Anatomy: The University of Texas Health Science Center. *Neuroscience Online*, 1997, Ch. 6.

"Are Smart Phones Spreading Faster than Any Technology in Human History?" by M. DeGusta. *MIT Technology Review*, May/June 2012.

"Be a Model Leader of Change" by D. Schneider and C. Goldwasser. *Management Review*, 1998, Vol. 87: 3.

"Change Fatigue" by J. Fitzell. *Professionals Australia* (Blog), 26 June 2015.

"Change Fatigue More Problematic than Senior Leaders May Think" by A. Stetzer. *Ketchum*, 14 Sept 2015.

"Creating a Culture of Learning in Six Steps" by B. Andreatta. *Lynda.com* Enterprise Solutions, Oct 2015.

"Eight Weeks to A Better Brain" by S. McGreevey. *Harvard Gazette*, 21 Jan 2011.

"Error Monitoring Using External Feedback: Specific Roles of the Habenular Complex, the Reward System, and the Cingulate Motor Area Revealed by Functional Magnetic Resonance Imaging" by M. Ullsperger and D. Von Cramon. *Journal of Neuroscience*, 2003, Vol. 23, p. 4308–14.

"Grasping the Intentions of Others with One's Own Mirror Neuron System" by M. Iacoboni et al. *PLOS (Public Library of Science) Biology*, 2005, Vol. 3:3, p. 79.

"Human Emotion and Memory: Interactions of the Amygdala and Hippocampal Complex" by E. Phelps. *Current Opinion in Neurobiology*, 2004, Vol. 14, p. 198–202.

"Jobs, Careers, and Callings: People's Relations to Their Work" by A. Wrzesniewski et al. *Journal of Research in Personality*, 1997, p. 21–3.

"Learned Helplessness" by M. Seligman. *Annual Review of Medicine*, 1972, Vol. 23: 1 p. 407–12.

"Measuring Meaningful Work: The Work and Meaning Inventory (WAMI)" by M. Steger et al. *Journal of Career Assessment*, 2010, p. 322–37.

"Mindfulness Practice Leads to Increases in Regional Brain Gray Matter Density" by B. Hölzel, et al. *Psychiatry Research*, 2011, Vol. 191: 1.

"Most Change Initiatives Fail—But They Don't Have To" by D. Leonard and C. Coltea. *Gallup Business Journal*, 24 May 2013.

"Neuroscience Reveals the Secrets of Meditation's Benefits" by M. Ricard, A. Lutz, and R. Davidson. *Scientific American*, 2014, Vol. 311:5.

"Only One-Quarter of Employers Are Sustaining Gains from Change Management Initiatives, Towers Watson Survey Finds" by T. Watson. *Willis Towers Watson*, 29 Aug 2013.

"Rick Rescolara" Wikipedia, accessed 5 Dec 2016.

"Rick Rescolara—Saved 2,687 Lives on September 11" by C. Bos. *Awesome Stories*, 29 Aug 2013.

"Six Tips for Working with the Brain to Create Real Behavior Change" by B. Andreatta. *Talent Development*, 8 Sept 2015, p. 48–53.

"The Amygdala and Emotion" by M. Gallagher and A. Chiba. *Current Opinion in Neurobiology*, 1996, Vol. 6: 2, p. 221–7.

"The Grateful Brain: The Neuroscience of Giving Thanks" by A. Korb. *Psychology Today*, 20 Nov 2012.

"The Habenula: From Stress Evasion to Value–Based Decision-Making" by O. Hikosaka. *Nature Reviews Neuroscience*, July 2010, p. 503–513.

"The Mind's Mirror" by L. Winerman. *American Psychological Association*, 2005, Vol. 36: 9, p. 48.

"The Mirror-Neuron System" by G. Rizzolatti and L. Craighero. *Annual Review of Neuroscience*, 2004, Vol. 27, p.169–92.

"The Pace of Technology Adoption Is Speeding Up" by R. McGrath. *Harvard Business Review*, 25 Nov 2013.

"The Power of Process" by K. Bobinet. *Experience Life*, Jan/Feb 2016.

"SCARF: A Brain-Based Model for Collaborating with and Influencing Others" by D. Rock. *NeuroLeadership Journal*, Jan 2008.

"SCARF: Lead in a Way That Will Engage People's Mind" by M. Bosman. *Strategic Leadership Institute*, 24 July 2012.

"Six Actions to Reduce and Prevent Change Fatigue" by D-M. Turner. *Turner Change Management, Inc.*, 1 Mar 2016.

"Symptoms of Change Fatigue" by D. Lock. *Daniel Lock Consulting.* 26 Nov 2015.

"What Are the Signs and Symptoms of Problem Sleepiness?" by National Heart, Lung, and Blood Institute, *National Institutes of Health*, 12 Feb 2012.

"What Google Learned from Its Quest to Build the Perfect Team" by C. Duhigg. *New York Times*, 28 Feb 2016.

"Where Am I? Where Am I Going?" by M-B. Moser and E. Moser. *Scientific American*, 2016, Vol. 313:1.

Books

Change Monster: The Human Forces That Fuel or Foil Corporate Transformation and Change by Jeanie Daniel Duck (Crown Business, 2001).

Conscious Capitalism: Liberating the Heroic Spirit of Business by John Mackey and Rajendra Sisodia (*Harvard Business Review*, 2013).

Conscious Business: How to Build Value Through Values by Fred Kofman (Sounds True, 2006).

Daring Greatly: How the Courage to Be Vulnerable Transforms the Way We Live, Love, Parent and Lead by Brené Brown (Gotham 2012; Avery, 2015).

Drive: The Surprising Truth about What Motivates Us by Daniel Pink (Riverhead Books, 2011).

Emotional Intelligence: Why It Can Matter More than IQ by Daniel Goleman (Bantam, 1995).

Flourish: A Visionary New Understanding of Happiness and Well-Being by Martin Seligman (Free Press, 2011).

Firms of Endearment: How World Class Companies Profit from Passion and Purpose by Rajendra Sisodia, David Wolfe and Jagdish Sheth (2nd edition, Pearson, 2014).

Holacracy: The New Management System For a Rapidly Changing World by Brian Robertson (Henry Holt & Co., 2015).

How Full Is Your Bucket? by Tom Rath and Donald Clifton (Gallup Press, 2004).

Into Thin Air: A Personal Account of the Mount Everest Disaster by Jon Krakauer (Villard Books, 1997).

Learned Helplessness: A Theory for the Age of Personal Control by Chris Peterson, Steven Maier, and Martin Seligman (Oxford University Press, 1995).

Managing Transitions: Making the Most of Change by William and Susan Bridges (3rd edition, Da Capo Lifelong Books, 2009).

Mindfulness: The New Science of Health and Happiness by The Editors of Time (Time: Special Edition, 2016).

Mindset: The New Psychology of Success by Carol Dweck (Random House, 2008).

On Death and Dying: What the Dying Have to Teach Doctors, Nurses, Clergy, and Their Own Families by E. Kubler-Ross (Simon & Schuster, 1969).

Reinventing Organizations: A Guide to Creating Organizations Inspired by the Next Stage of Human Consciousness by Frederic Laloux (Nelson Parker, 2014).

Rising Strong: The Reckoning. The Rumble. The Revolution. by Brené Brown (Spiegel & Grau, 2015).

Search Inside Yourself: The Unexpected Path to Achieving Success, Happiness (and World Peace) by Chade-Meng Tan (HarperOne, 2012).

Start with Why: How Great Leaders Inspire Everyone to Take Action by Simon Sinek (Portfolio, 2009).

Start Something That Matters by Blake Mycoskie (Spiegel & Grau, 2011).

Switch: How to Change Things When Change Is Hard by Chip and Dan Heath (Crown Business, 2010).

The Climb: Tragic Ambitions on Everest by Anatoli Boukreev and G. Weston DeWalt (St. Martin's Press, 1997).

The Emotional Life of Your Brain: How Its Unique Patterns Affect the Way You Think, Feel, and Live—and How You Can Change Them by Richard Davidson and Sharon Begley (Hudson Street Press, 2012).

The Four Disciplines of Execution: Achieving Your Wildly Important Goals by Chris McChesney, Sean Covey, and Jim Huling (Free Press, 2012).

The Meditative Mind: The Varieties of Meditative Experience by Daniel Goleman (TarcherPerigee, 1996).

The Power of Habit: Why We Do What We Do in Life and Business by Charles Duhigg (Random House, 2012).

The Purpose Economy: How Your Desire for Impact, Personal Growth and Community Is Changing the World by Aaron Hurst (2nd edition, Elevate, 2016).

Thinking, Fast and Slow by Daniel Kahneman (Farrar, Straus and Giroux, 2013).

We First: How Brands and Consumers Use Social Media to Build a Better World by Simon Mainwaring (St. Martin's Press, 2011).

Wired to Grow: Harness the Power of Brain Science to Master Any Skill by Britt Andreatta (7th Mind Publishing, 2015).

Guides

- *Employee Recognition Report 2015* (from Globoforce.com)
- *Predictions for 2016 Bersin Research Report* (from Deloitte.com)
- *2016 Workforce Purpose Index* (from Imperative.com)
- *State of the American Workplace* (from Gallup.com)
- *State of the Global Workplace* (from Gallup.com)
- *The Global and Real Time State of Employee Engagement 2016* (from Officevibe.com)

Media

"Drive: The Surprising Truth about What Motivates Us" by Dan Pink (RSA Animates, 2010; www.thersa.org/discover/videos/rsa-animate/2010/04/rsa-animate---drive).

"Empathy" by Brené Brown (RSA Animates, 2013; www.thersa.org/discover/videos/rsa-shorts/2013/12/Brene-Brown-on-Empathy).

"Having Difficult Conversations" by Britt Andreatta (Lynda.com, 2013; www.lynda.com/Business-Skills-tutorials/Having-Difficult-Conversations/124085-2.html).

"Leading with Emotional Intelligence" by Britt Andreatta (Lynda.com, 2013; www.lynda.com/Business-Skills-tutorials/Leading-Emotional-Intelligence/124087-2.html).

"Leading Change" by Britt Andreatta (Lynda.com, 2013; www.lynda.com/Business-Skills-tutorials/Leading-Organizational-Change/133350-2.html).

"Listening to Shame" by Brené Brown (TED Talk, 2012; www.ted.com/talks/brene_brown_listening_to_shame).

"Potential: How Your Past Hijacks Your Future" by Britt Andreatta (TEDx Talk, 2014, www.youtube.com/watch?v=yXt_70Ak670).

The Croods (DreamWorks, 2013).

"The Neurons That Shaped Civilization" by Vilaynur Ramachandran (TED Talk, 2010; www.ted.com/talks/vs_ramachandran_the_neurons_that_shaped_civilization).

"The Power of Habit: How Target Knows You Better Than You Do" by Charles Duhigg (Columbia Business School, 2013; www.youtube.com/watch?v=0G_beU-SmLw).

"The Power of Vulnerability" by Brené Brown (TEDx Houston, 2010; www.ted.com/talks/brene_brown_on_vulnerability).

"The Neuroscience of Learning" by Britt Andreatta (Lynda.com course, 2014; www.lynda.com/Education-Higher-Education-tutorials/Neuroscience-Learning/188434-2.html).

Websites, Tools, and Centers

- Calculating ROI of Happiness (from DeliveringHappiness.com) deliveringhappiness.com/services/calculate-your-roi
- Center for Appreciative Inquiry www.centerforappreciativeinquiry.net
- Center for Investigating Healthy Minds (University of Wisconsin) www.investigatinghealthyminds.org/cihmcenter.html
- Consortium for Research on Emotional Intelligence in Organizations (Rutgers University) www.eiconsortium.org
- Foundation for a Mindful Society www.mindful.org/about-mindful
- Great Place to Work www.greatplacetowork.com
- Re:Work (from Google.com) rework.withgoogle.com
- Neuroscience Research Center (University of Texas) med.uth.edu/nrc
- What Does Employee Turnover Cost You? (from Bonus.com) bonus.ly/cost-of-employee-turnover-calculator
- Wired to Resist (companion tools and training materials) www.BrittAndreatta.com/wired-to-resist

Acknowledgments. Practicing Gratitude

I dedicate this book to my mother, who made her transition September 14, 2016. She was a smart, strong, and resilient woman who survived many difficult challenges. She taught me so much about what it means to live, love, and laugh. When I was growing up, we lived through a lot of change, moving nearly every year. As she always said, "Home is where you feed the cat." Indeed.

This book was cocreated with my amazing team. My deep gratitude goes to Jenefer Angell (PassionfruitProjects.com), my editor and friend, who consistently uplevels my ideas while keeping my voice intact (me, but better!). Special thanks to the wonderful Leah Young (Leah-Young.com) who takes my wonky sketches and creates beautiful illustrations. So happy for the wonderful teams at Dog Ear Publishing and 7th Mind Publishing. You are rock stars!

Blessings for my dear friends and soul sisters, Lisa Slavid, and Kelly McGill, for their great input on this book and for helping the world become more teal.

I am so fortunate to have lots of support and love in my life. Hugs and kisses to Chris, Kiana, Dana, Pema, Mike, Barbara, Roger, Kendra, Carole, Jan, Cherie, Cody, and Ellie. A special shout-out to my circle of "power women"—Dawn, Elaine, and Lisa—for holding space and cheering me on.

To my tribe of learning and leadership professionals: we are in the business of cultivating the potential of our people and I am honored to share this important work with you.

Here's to the power of yet!

About the Author

Dr. Britt Andreatta knows how to harness human potential. Drawing on her unique background in leadership, psychology, education, and the human sciences, she has a profound understanding of how to unlock the best in people.

A seasoned professional with more than 25 years of experience working with thousands of people, her research and experience consulting with businesses, government agencies, universities, and nonprofit organizations have allowed her to create powerful solutions to today's workplace challenges.

Her published titles on learning and leadership include *Wired to Grow*, *The Neuroscience of Learning*, *Leading Change*, *Having Difficult Conversations*, and *Leading with Emotional Intelligence*, to name a few. Britt is currently writing several more books. A highly sought-after speaker, Britt speaks frequently at international conferences and delivered a TEDx talk called "How Your Past Hijacks Your Future" to rave reviews.

Dr. Andreatta has served as professor and dean at the University of California, Antioch University, and several graduate schools, where she has won numerous teaching awards including "Professor of the Year." She regularly consults with executives and organizations on how to maximize their full potential, including several Fortune 500 and 100 companies.

Britt has won many international awards including the 2016 Global Training & Development Leadership Award from the World Training & Development Congress. She won the Gold Medal for *Chief Learning Officer* magazine's prestigious Trailblazer Award for the leadership development program she designed and was also nominated for the CLO Strategy Award for her work on a groundbreaking performance management program based on the growth mindset.

Britt is currently an author for Lynda.com/LinkedInLearning.com. She is the former Chief Learning Officer for Lynda.com, where she designed and implemented professional development programs for all global employees, ranging from individual contributors to executive coaching. Dr. Andreatta also served as the Senior Learning Consultant for Global Talent and Leadership Development at LinkedIn.

She is now focused full-time on her consulting practice while continuing to write books and speak at events around the world. To learn more, visit the following sites.

Website: www.BrittAndreatta.com

LinkedIn: www.LinkedIn.com/in/BrittAndreatta

Twitter: @BrittAndreatta

YouTube: www.youtube.com/c/BrittAndreatta

Taking These Ideas Beyond the Page

If you are interested in bringing the Change Journey Model to your organization, Britt Andreatta has created a range of materials to help you. Her engaging keynotes, presentations, and workshops challenge assumptions and move audiences to action. Learn more by visiting www.BrittAndreatta.com/Wired-to-Resist.

CPSIA information can be obtained
at www.ICGtesting.com
Printed in the USA
BVHW070922091218
534986BV00032B/615/P